Grown Ups

A PLAY

by

Jules Feiffer

SAMUEL FRENCH

FOUNDED 1830

New York Hollywood London Toronto

WWW.SAMUELFRENCH.COM

Opening Night December 10, 1981

LYCEUM THEATRE

A Shubert Organization Theatre

Gerald Schoenfeld, *Chairman*   Bernard B. Jacobs, *President*

MIKE NICHOLS AND EMANUEL AZENBERG
WITH THE SHUBERT ORGANIZATION
PRESENT

BOB
DISHY

FRANCES   HAROLD
STERNHAGEN   GOULD

IN

JULES FEIFFER'S

A NEW PLAY

WITH

**CHERYL   KATE   JENNIFER
GIANNINI   McGREGOR-STEWART   DUNDAS**

SETTINGS BY   COSTUMES BY   LIGHTING BY
ANDREW JACKNESS   DUNYA RAMICOVA   PAUL GALLO

DIRECTED BY

JOHN MADDEN

PRODUCED BY EMANUEL AZENBERG AND MIKE NICHOLS
in association with WAYNE M. ROGERS
Originally Produced by The American Repertory Theatre, Cambridge, Massachusetts

CAST
(in order of appearance)

Helen .... FRANCES STERNHAGEN

Jack .... HAROLD GOULD

Marilyn .... KATE McGREGOR-STEWART

Jake .... BOB DISHY

Louise .... CHERYL GIANNINI

Edie .... JENNIFER DUNDAS

THERE WILL BE AN INTERMISSION AFTER ACT ONE
AND A PAUSE BETWEEN ACTS TWO AND THREE.

1. The Present. Marilyn's Kitchen in New Rochelle
2. One Year Later. Jake and Louise's Apartment in New York
3. The Following Sunday. Jake and Louise's Apartment

STANDBYS

Standbys never substitute for listed players unless specific notification
is made at the time of performance.

For Jake—Stephen D. Newman
For Helen—Georgine Hall
For Louise & Marilyn—Barbara Eda-Young
For Edie—Shelly Inglis

CHARACTERS

HELEN — Jake's mother

JACK — Jake's father

MARILYN — Jake's sister

JAKE

LOUISE — Jake's wife

EDIE — Jake's daughter

CHARACTER NOTES

The characters in this play suffer from unrequited need. Love exists in them, but it is ill-conceived and badly translated.

The strongest among them, Helen, cannot be played as a stereotypical stage or t.v. Jewish mother or the play sinks like a stone. She derives from another, less familiar tradition. Her style is cheerful; she has cultivated a genteel, educated, ladylike manner. Her forays into Yiddishisms, while used fondly, have a touch of condescension. Her flirtatiousness and playfulness are conscious choices, done for effect. Her power is innate, rarely calling for naked display.

She is the motor of Act 1 as Jake is the motor of Acts 2 and 3.

Jake is the master of family sleight of hand; now you see him, now you don't. He has spent a lifetime sidestepping confrontation, joking, kidding, getting his way through charm, distance, outlasting or ignoring the opposition; quick on his feet in family situations.

Louise's manner with Jake in Act 2 is vulnerable, combative but defensive. Later, with his family, she covers up: flirtatious with Jack, teasing and provocative with Helen.

Grown Ups

ACT ONE

TIME: *Present. The scene is* MARILYN'S *kitchen in New
Rochelle, midday. A windowed door leads out to
the garden where a birthday party is in progress.
Through that and other windows we see trees in full
bloom and hear party noises. The kitchen table and
counter is laden with platters of food: chicken
salad, potato salad, chopped liver, etc.* JACK *and*
HELEN, *both in their 60's, stand at the garden door,
looking out.*

HELEN and JACK. (*With* MARILYN *offstage and*
OTHER OFFSTAGE VOICES. *Sing.*)
Happy birthday to you;
Happy birthday to you.
Happy birthday, dear Rudy;
Happy birthday to you. (HELEN *moves Downstage into
the kitchen, followed by* JACK. MARILYN *enters from
garden, carrying a tray of dirty plates and dishes.*)
    HELEN. I marvel at your efficiency, Marilyn. Never in
a million years could I put on this kind of shindig.
    OFFSTAGE SHOUT. Food! More food! We're dying out
here!
    MARILYN. (*Shouts.*) Suffer! (*Grabs an onion and
knife, sits at the kitchen table and starts slicing it rapid-
ly.*) This you gotta hear! I was coming home Wednesday on the bus from Philadelphia—(HELEN *rises and
crosses to oven.*)
    JACK. Nobody said a word to me about Philadelphia.

7

HELEN. Marilyn, you want me to check the chicken for you?

MARILYN. Leave it, Mama.

HELEN. The old lady's trying to give a hand.

MARILYN. I'm like you; if somebody starts to help I forget what I'm doing. Sit down, you'll love this: I was coming home from Philadelphia—

JACK. (*To* HELEN.) Did you know she was out of town?

MARILYN. Two days!

JACK. Who took care of my grandchildren?

MARILYN. How should I know? Out of sight, out of mind. No, Rudy was here. He got them out of bed in the morning and back in bed at night. In between I don't even want to know what happened. Am I ever going to be able to tell you this or not?

HELEN. (*Returning to table.*) You're going out of town, Marilyn?

MARILYN. No, Mama, I'm back.

HELEN. And we weren't even told?

JACK. Not a single word!

HELEN. You shouldn't go away without telling us, Marilyn. Did you have a good time?

MARILYN. Terrific. It was a social work conference.

JACK. It's not my idea of a good time.

HELEN. Is there a draft in here? Who'd have believed it? My daughter at a convention. I bet she was the life of the party! Did you make a speech, Marilyn? "My fellow Americans, 'Shoot if you must this old gray head, but spare your country's flag,' she said."

MARILYN. Believe me, it was a refreshing change. There they let me talk!

HELEN. Where's Jake?

MARILYN. On the way. So I caught the last bus back to the city—

JACK. I don't like you taking a last bus, it's dangerous.

MARILYN. It's not nearly as dangerous as trying to tell a story around here.

JACK. Riding alone in a bus at night. Why didn't you take the train?

MARILYN. To tell you the truth, right now I'm sorry I went.

HELEN. (*Wandering about kitchen.*) Jack, mmmmmm, look at all these doings! A miracle worker, my daughter! A veritable feast!

JACK. Rudy doesn't deserve it, even if it is his birthday Am I right or am I right, Marilyn?

MARILYN. I don't believe it! How is it Jake can tell a story, Mama can tell a story — but as long as I live I have never been able to get you two to listen to one of my stories?

JACK. Do you know what she's talking about?

HELEN. You want to tell us a story? I'm all ears.

MARILYN. Forget it! I don't want to anymore.

HELEN. Did you ever!

MARILYN. It's true! You never want to hear my stories.

JACK. That's the most ridiculous thing I ever heard of!

HELEN. Marilyn, you're over-excited because of the party. You've worked wonders! I mean it. I doff my chapeau. Where's my chapeau? Has anyone seen my chapeau? O.K., you will have to imagine it. That's an order! (*Mimes the tipping of a hat.*)

JACK. (*Laughs.*) The way she does it I can swear I almost see it!

HELEN. Now we'll sit and listen. Tell your story. (*Sits.*)

MARILYN. I'm out of the mood.

HELEN. Moods yet! She's getting to be as bad as Jake!

OFFSTAGE SHOUT. Marilyn! We're dying!

MARILYN. (*Shouts.*) You'll survive!

HELEN. Wherever do you have time for so many talented people? Architects, lawyers, pischologists — (JACK *laughs.*) I rot a new poem. Did I tell you?

JACK. First we're going to hear Marilyn's story.

MARILYN. No, no, I want to hear Mama's poem.

JACK. Fair's fair.

MARILYN. Sorry, you missed your chance. Mama!

HELEN. It's too silly.

JACK. She has to be coaxed.

MARILYN. Then forget it, I got too much to do.

HELEN. How can I resist? A-hem! (*Recites.*)
I'm sittin' here wishin'
The electrician would stop drilling the walls and would leave
— (This is last week, they came in on us, Marilyn, not a word of warning, tore the apartment apart.) —
The rain of plaster
Is like a disaster,
I tremor in each sleeve.
If only it weren't
That we needed strong current
The house would be tidy and quiet
But now we're upset
And the end is not yet
On his own home
the landlord should try it.

JACK. Damn clever!

HELEN. Jake's not the only talented member of this family. You like my opus?

MARILYN. Sure, Mama.

HELEN. Tell your brother Jake he'd better look to his

laurels if his Ma gets going one of these days. I have high hopus for my opus.

MARILYN. (*On her way out the kitchen door with food platters.*) They'll all be disappointed if you don't come outside.

HELEN. Tell them the party's in here. (MARILYN *exits.*) She's such a hard worker. It takes my breath away.

JACK. She has what it takes!

HELEN. It's too much excitement for me. I can't take it. Maybe we should have entertained more.

JACK. We had more than enough company.

HELEN. The children's friends. That was a scene!

JACK. Just the way I like it. Nobody needed an invitation!

HELEN. They ate and drank us out of house and home. The old woman in the shoe, your old lady. And how jealous Jake used to get! "I bring my friends home and they end up talking to you!" Such aggravation! How much will you bet me *she's* not coming with him.

JACK. Don't be silly!

HELEN. As usual, your head's in the sand.

JACK. According to you, if my head's not in the clouds it's in the sand. If it's ever on my shoulders don't forget to let me know.

HELEN. Forget? I'll throw a party! I'm not saying she's not a wonderful girl. I only wish Jake would sometime put his foot down. He's still not too old for a little advice from the old lady. How often did he come to us, one wild scheme after another?

JACK. He's all talk. Half the time he doesn't mean a thing.

HELEN. Jack, you've got a heart of gold but when you fall down on the job you really know how to do it.

(*Silence between them.* HELEN *wanders about kitchen.*)

MARILYN. (*Enters with tray full of dirty glasses.*) Ta-da! Jake has finally made an appearance! (*Crosses to oven and takes out chicken.*)

HELEN. (*To* JACK.) The hostess with the mostes'!

JACK. Where's that granddaughter of mine? I can't wait to get my hands on her!

HELEN. Your Pa and his grandchildren! It's positively indecent!

MARILYN. Louise and the baby have colds.

HELEN. They're not sick!

JACK. I should've known it!

HELEN. They have a temperature?

MARILYN. It never dawned on me to ask.

HELEN. Marilyn, don't let me hear you sound off with a suspicious mind.

MARILYN. Mama, you know as well as I do—

HELEN. I know people get sick. I'm sick all the time. Do you get mad at me?

MARILYN. Plenty!

JACK. Ask a foolish question!

HELEN. I don't like it—a baby that age being sick so often.

MARILYN. Don't worry, it's limited to birthdays and get-togethers.

JACK. She has a point.

HELEN. Jake's all right?

MARILYN. He's outside.

JACK. So where is he?

MARILYN. Talking to Rudy. If you feel better, come out.

JACK. Fashionably late. The big shot! You think he'll write a front page story for the *New York Times* on your party?

MARILYN. Some story we'd make.

JACK. Let him come in and interview his father.

HELEN. Maybe I'll stretch my legs in the garden for a while.

JACK. Relax. We got the whole day before us.

HELEN. (*Rises.*) Marilyn says it's sunny. It might do us both a world of good. (*To* MARILYN.) I don't know what's the matter with me lately, Marilyn. No get up and go. Your old lady's becoming a stick in the mud.

MARILYN. Come on, Daddy. Neither of you has ever taken a look at my garden.

JACK. Have Jake come and escort me and I'll pay tribute to your garden.

MARILYN. Look, just for once—

JACK. I demand an honor guard of my son. I hold a venerable position at this party. I am the senior member.

MARILYN. O.K., I don't want you to see my garden. I'll send him in.

JACK. Don't trouble yourself. He'll eventually get around to it.

HELEN. You don't want to see Marilyn's gladiolas?

JACK. I wouldn't know a gladiola from a palm tree. You go if you want to, Helen. I'll have a drink.

HELEN. (*Sits.*) What's the big hurry?

JACK. It's perfectly all right.

HELEN. It makes no never mind to me. Marilyn, I was in Woolworth's yesterday. I went shopping and overdid it. I took it easy but still I got all tuckered out. So I stopped for a chocolate milkshake in Woolworth's. A young woman was sitting on the stool next door to me. So proud, she musta thunk she was in Longchamps. You should have seen her put away a hot dog and roll. As if it were caviar. Well, my deah! I had to hold back the tears of laughter. She took out a silver-plated cigarette case that must have cost her boyfriend an arm and a leg. Then she turned to me and asked for a match. Me, she's asking! Then she asked the waitress, then the busboy, then another customer who asked another customer who asked another. I was in convulsions! Not a single match in all of Woolworth's! She looked like she was about to have apoplexy.

MARILYN. (*Laughing.*) Mama, how do you find them? (*Exits with trays of food.*)

JACK. (*To* MARILYN.) Tell him the liquor's in here! That'll bring him fast enough!

HELEN. (*To* MARILYN.) Me, I'm an innocent. They find me! (*To* JACK.) I wish you wouldn't talk like that.

JACK. Marilyn? She's a good sport.

HELEN. You know what I mean.

JACK. What? I'll offend your son, the teetotaler?

HELEN. Who sets the example?

JACK. That's the most ridiculous thing I ever heard.

HELEN. I know where you keep the bottle. On the sixth shelf where you think I can't reach it.

JACK. Don't be silly.

HELEN. Behind William Shirer. I'm on to your tricks, young man. I know you from the old country. (JAKE *enters.*)

JAKE. Everyone's outside. And you're inside. (JAKE, *well dressed, in his 30's, hugs and pecks both his* PARENTS. HELEN *returns the embrace warmly, clutching him for a long time, till* JAKE *must detach himself gently.* JACK *starts to respond casually but, overcome with sudden emotion, grabs him and kisses him on both cheeks.*) Come on! The party's outside!

HELEN. Not us, kid!

JACK. We're the party! You son of a gun! I'm mad as hell at you! Where's my granddaughter?

HELEN. Look at him, you look skinny.

JAKE. Louise caught cold, now Edie's got it.

HELEN. Do they have a temperature, sonny?

JAKE. It's just a cold, Mama.

HELEN. Tell Louise not to fool around. Take the baby's temperature.

JAKE. O.K., I'll tell her.

HELEN. Don't say you'll tell her, really tell her.

JAKE. I'll tell her you told me to tell her.

HELEN. I can't get to first base with him.

JACK. You're late enough. The day's half gone.

JAKE. But now I'm here. Feast your eyes!

HELEN. You on a diet?

JAKE. Burp!

HELEN. You look like you lost weight. Are you taking care of yourself?

JAKE. Not if I can help it.

HELEN. Don't clown! You have too much illness in your family. I don't like it one little bit.

JAKE. (*Hands them two pictures on oak tag paper.*) To you from Edie. She drew these for you.

JACK. How do you like that? Mom, will you look at this?

HELEN. This is mine? Is this for me, Jake?

JAKE. All yours!

HELEN. It's remarkable, sonny boy! Did anybody help her?

JAKE. She did it all by herself.

HELEN. The trees and everything? Jake, she has talent!

JACK. It brings tears to my eyes! (HELEN *and* JACK *compare pictures.*) It looks just like me!

JAKE. That's funny, it's supposed to be a cow.

JACK. I can't believe it! 8 years old! She's got what it takes, all right!

HELEN. Our neighbors, the Robinsons, have the loveliest daughter who does the most accomplished water colors. They'd knock your eyes out! Tell Louise she must save all her drawings. You never know how valuable these may be some day! How do you like that stuff, Dad? Collectors' items! (SHE *notices* JAKE *noticing his* FATHER *as* HE *nervously scratches the backs of his hands.*) His hands are giving him trouble again.

JACK. Go on!

HELEN. He doesn't eat.

JACK. *You* don't eat.

HELEN. I eat what's good for me. But you! You leave all the food on your plate. He's still a picky eater, your old man. The two of you. I had my hands full. Special orders from their highnesses! I remember when you were four, the doctor bawled me out that I wasn't feeding you enough. I took you home in the subway, I felt every eye was on me, accusing fingers—(*Points.*) child murderer! I got you home, sat you down and stuffed food down your throat. You spit it up and I stuffed it down again. What did I know? I was terrified!

JAKE. *You* were terrified?

HELEN. Such a dope, your mother. To this day I wonder if that's what made you a picky eater. I wake up sometimes in the middle of the night worrying about it. Heart palpitations. I'm getting over-excited now just talking about it.

JAKE. Don't worry, Mama, I lived.

HELEN. What did I know? The mistakes I made with you! Jake, you shoulda picked yourself another Ma. You don't hold it agin, me, sonny boy?

JAKE. I forgive you, Ma. You know me: a Christ-like figure. Turn the other cheek.

HELEN. You turn your cheek to me, I'll stick an

enema in it. Remember, young man, I yam a mother!
(JACK *laughs,* JAKE *smiles.*) I yam what I yam! Oh, how
the three of us could cut up! The four of us, Marilyn
too. All those bedtime carryings on in the kitchen!
(*Rises and clasps her hands to her breast, sings
Gershwin's* Funny Face *to* JAKE.)
"I love your funny face
Your sunny, funny face
For you're a cutie
With more than beauty
You've got a lot of personality,
For me
You fill the world with smiles
For miles and miles and miles
Though you're no handsome Harry,
For worlds I'd not replace
You sunny, funny face."

JACK. More! More! (HELEN *does a little dance, a
kick, wiggles her ass.* JACK *laps it up, applauds, cries
"Bravo!"* JAKE *goes to the bar and pours himself a
drink.*)

HELEN. (*Sits.*) The old gray mare, she ain't what she
used to be. (*To* JAKE.) How many does that make?

JAKE. I lost count hours ago. I'm kidding. This is my
first.

HELEN. Some joke. Does Louise drink that poison?

JAKE. Only to excess.

HELEN. Some fun, huh, kid? You can't for once
please your poor old mother?

JAKE. You want one, Dad?

HELEN. For my sake, sonny boy. You're a wonderful
person, you have a wonderful family, you have a
wonderful career. I don't want you to do anything to
bring sorrow into your life. Believe me, I know what I'm

talking about. (JACK *fidgets,* JAKE *puts drink down.*) Thank you, sonny dearest. Pour it down the sink like a good fellow.

JAKE. It's not necessary, Ma.

HELEN. I don't have the breath to argue.

JAKE. Look, I'm not going to pour it down the sink.

HELEN. You won't do that one little thing more for me?

JAKE. The one thing more I did for you is to not have a drink.

HELEN. Not for me, darling boy, for you.

JAKE. I'll pour it back in the bottle.

HELEN. So someone else can drink the poison. Don't do me any favors. (JAKE *pours drink into bottle, spilling some on the table.* HELEN *wipes it up with the flat of her hand.*)

JACK. So what's the good word, young-fellow-me-lad? When are they going to make you editor of the *Times*?

JAKE. Oh, I didn't tell you? They fired me.

JACK. My son, the comedian. Anything new to report?

JAKE. You see my story yesterday on the dangerous drugs U.S. corporations are selling in the Third World?

JACK. Did I see it? I cut it out and Scotch taped it to the cash register. Any customer who came into the store, I wouldn't sell him a shirt until he read your report. Lucky for me it was a short article or I'd be out good money.

JAKE. Well, they hacked it to pieces.

JACK. What'd they hack? Your article?

JAKE. I turned in 25 hundred words, and short at that for all the information I had to stuff in. They butchered it. They simply butchered it.

JACK. They have to make room for someone else in the paper besides you, Jake.

HELEN. They have their own fish to fry; I'm sure they know what they're doing.

JACK. What else is new? You working on anything special?

JAKE. I'm doing an article for *Esquire* on Henry Kissinger.

JACK. How do you like that! Are you going to get to meet him?

JAKE. I interviewed him yesterday.

JACK. As I live and breathe! Ma, did you hear that?

HELEN. Why not? Someday Henry Kissinger will interview Jake.

JACK. What else is new.

JAKE. Well, I don't know — I wasn't going to tell you: I'm in the middle of working on a book.

HELEN. Your own book! Day and night he's at it!

JACK. How do you like that! How do you like that! What on?

JAKE. It's a study, a social study, an analysis, O.K.? Of the aberrant effects of cold war politics on the state of our domestic lives.

HELEN. My son, Walter Lippmann!

JAKE. We're living in an age of institutionalized paranoia today — O.K.? — an extraordinary sense of powerlessness from the guy on the assembly line in Detroit to those clowns in the White House. Don't get nervous, Ma, listen. So I think I can trace the roots of this back to the cold war — not in terms of foreign policy — but how it's corrupted our national spirit. O.K?, what I'm writing about — it's a wonderful story — the moral and ethical disintegration of the American Dream, basically.

HELEN. You don't want to get into trouble, Jake.

JACK. Don't be silly. It's a damned clever idea. Where did you get it from? Kissinger?

HELEN. They're very powerful men. I want you to be careful.

JACK. Listen to her worry.

HELEN. You've got responsibilities. You're not foot-loose, you know.

JACK. You have a publisher?

JAKE. I want to get into it before I start looking.

HELEN. You shouldn't do something for nothing.

JAKE. Well, I can't very well sell a book that doesn't have a line written, Ma.

HELEN. You don't have to use that tone of voice; I know a thing or two. Authors get advances all the time. You have a considerable reputation. Any publisher should be dying to get his hands on you.

JACK. What else?

HELEN. Haven't we heard enough? He's a dynamo, my son. The day you got the job the excitement in your voice when you told us over the telephone. Dad and I sat up half the night in the kitchen toasting your success with glasses of milk. We were big shots! Our son on the *New York Times*!

JACK. When are we going to see you?

JAKE. You're seeing me right now.

JACK. Don't be a wise guy. When are you coming to visit? I have hopes of seeing my granddaughter before I die.

JAKE. Dad, whenever I see you, you ask when am I going to see you? I really don't know what you want. You want me to move back in? (*Pause.*) You know how often most other sons visit their parents?

JACK. I didn't know there was a standard.

JAKE. Look, I'm here. We're together. Let's try to enjoy it.

JACK. I'd enjoy it if I could for once see my granddaughter.

JAKE. Anytime! You come over anytime you want. How many times do I have to tell you that?

JACK. That's not an invitation.

JAKE. It is an invitation.

JACK. An invitation is next Tuesday, next Wednesday, next Sunday. That's an invitation.

JAKE. That's your house. In my house we don't believe in formalities like that.

JACK. In his house! Your friends all drop in just like that? You don't make Friday dates, Saturday dates? They just call and say "We're coming over"?

JAKE. That's right.

JACK. You're full of hot air!

JAKE. It's true.

JACK. I'll tell you what's true. When you give us a date to come over we'll come over.

JAKE. What do you want? A formal invitation?

HELEN. It's been heard of.

JACK. You could also come see us.

JAKE. I do.

JACK. With the family.

JAKE. Louise had a very difficult miscarriage.

JACK. Three years ago and she's still having her miscarriage.

HELEN. Seriously, Jake, are you not telling us something?

JAKE. She's all right. She just can't travel much.

HELEN. You're not protecting us from bad news? Don't ever protect us.

JAKE. She's fine. Just not very strong.

JACK. Now tell us you didn't take her to Europe.

JAKE. That was on assignment.

JACK. Pretend for once that we're your assignment.

HELEN. She didn't have to leave the baby with strangers.

JAKE. She didn't leave the baby — *we* left the baby. I'm the father, remember? We left the baby with Annie.

HELEN. I don't mean to question Louise's judgment.

JAKE. Mama, it was both our judgment. Annie has been with us since Edie was born. She has two kids of her own and she's very responsible. Maybe next time we'll leave her with you.

JACK. Maybe. Maybe means there won't be a next time.

HELEN. What is it, Jake? Is there anything about your marriage I should know about you're not telling me?

JAKE. Absolutely not!

HELEN. You're getting along?

JAKE. Perfectly!

HELEN. Whatever other trouble there is in the family I'd rather have you happy. That comes first.

JAKE. I am happy.

HELEN. Good.

JACK. Fine. Everybody's happy. When do I see my granddaughter?

JAKE. Look, Louise has had very bad experiences of her own with families. You know that.

HELEN. Our fault, I suppose.

JAKE. It's not your fault. She just doesn't go in for family gatherings. It has nothing to do with you.

HELEN. She's a little cold, your wife. I'm more sorry than I can tell you to say it.

JAKE. She is not cold, Mama. I won't have you talk about my wife behind her back.

HELEN. When else do I get the chance?

JACK. Show us her front and we'll talk about her. We'd be more than happy, I promise you!

HELEN. All we ask is a chance to know her better and love her. She'll find out: all you have is your family. Just wait when there's an emergency. Friends go this way, that way. All you have is your family.

JAKE. I've had lots of emergencies with Louise. She has always stood behind me. You don't know her. She has literally saved my life. More than once. You don't know how lucky I am to have her. She's the best thing that ever happened to me! (*A long, uncomfortable pause.*)

HELEN. Your welfare has always been uppermost in our minds.

JAKE. I haven't had a chance to talk to Rudy.

HELEN. Far be it from me—

JAKE. It is *his* birthday.

JACK. Marilyn said you already talked to him

JAKE. I said hello to him.

JACK. Say goodby to him. Who's stopping you?

JAKE. I won't be long.

JACK. Don't do us any favors. (*JAKE exits.*)

HELEN. I made some terrible mistakes with him. Marilyn turned out like a dream, but Jake—Can you believe it?

JACK. He's full of hot air.

HELEN. (*Simultaneously.*) I'm not going to let him make me sick.

MARILYN. (*Enters.*) You want anything?

HELEN. Peace of mind.

MARILYN. That I can't give you. How about some nice fish?

HELEN. You're too good. (*To JACK.*) She's too good.

MARILYN. You feel like coming outside now, Mama?

HELEN. I'm not up to it.

JACK. She's not up to it.

MARILYN. It's beautiful outside. You'll like it once you're out there. If you don't you can always come right back in.

HELEN. I don't have the strength. All this emotion! I think I overdid it with the cleaning yesterday.

JACK. She'll never learn.

HELEN. It had to be done.

JACK. I told you I would've done it.

HELEN. Later. Always later.

JACK. What's the big hurry?

HELEN. The big hurry is you do things in their proper place and then you're finished.

JACK. I would have done it.

HELEN. I didn't have the strength to keep after you. (*To* MARILYN.) He means well but you have to keep after him. (*Takes* MARILYN's *hand.*) Jake should have found someone like you, Marilyn. She would have put him on the right track. You made such a lovely home, my heart swells with pride. Rudy should know how lucky he is.

MARILYN. I'm lucky he puts up with me.

JACK. He's the lucky one. What are you talking about?

HELEN. The mistake is to let them get away with too much. They get to take too much for granted.

MARILYN. Ma, I'm not that easy to live with, believe me.

JACK. She doesn't know what she's talking about.

HELEN. You're a saint.

MARILYN. Please don't do that.

HELEN. What did I do now?

MARILYN. You don't call me a saint and I won't call you a virgin.

HELEN. Your mouth too? What did I do to deserve two such mouths?

MARILYN. Mama.

HELEN. I'm decent. My mother taught me to be decent. Dad, it's stuffy, please open a window.

MARILYN. Why don't you go outside?

HELEN. Do what I ask. I'm getting a flush.

MARILYN. I'll do it. (*Opens window.*) Is that too much air? (HELEN *doesn't answer.*) Mama? (HELEN *signals with a wave of her hand that* SHE *can't talk.*) Are you gonna be all right? Do you want anything? (HELEN, *with another wave of her hand, signals her away from the window, points to the chair* SHE *wants* MARILYN *to sit down in.* MARILYN *sits.* HELEN *waves her in closer.* MARILYN *moves close in on her.*)

HELEN. (*Whispers.*) I'll be all right in a second. (JACK *appears increasingly nervous, scratches the top of his hands.*) Tell your father not to pick.

MARILYN. Don't pick.

JACK. I'm scratching. (HELEN *starts to whisper, can't, shakes her head at* MARILYN *and then points to* JACK.)

MARILYN. She wants you to stop scratching. (HELEN *waves* MARILYN *in closer, whispers in her ear.*) She says you have a skin rash.

JACK. It's acting up.

MARILYN. Leave it alone. What are you doing for it?

JACK. It's O.K. I'll live.

MARILYN. Let me see. (HELEN *points for her to look.* MARILYN *looks.*) Daddy, they look awful!

JACK. (*Almost proud.*) They hurt like hell.

HELEN. I'm a little better.

MARILYN. Are you O.K., Mama? Can I get you

something?

HELEN. It was one of my flushes. They put me out of commission for a while. I'm all right. A little overheated.

MARILYN. You better relax. Take it easy.

HELEN. I could use a little air.

MARILYN. Why don't you cool off first?

HELEN. I'll cool off outside. I can't breathe in this stuffy kitchen. How do you put up with it?

MARILYN. I don't know if you should go out so soon.

HELEN. (*To* JACK.) Isn't she an angel? If it weren't for you I don't know what.

MARILYN. You need help?

HELEN. That'll be the day! (*Starts off.* JACK *falls in behind her, scratching his hands.* MARILYN *collapses into a chair and pours herself a drink. Sips it and lets go of a sigh.* JAKE *enters.*)

JAKE. Drinking, Marilyn? (*Puts his hand to his heart.*) It hurts me right here.

MARILYN. (*Turns to see him.*) I was scared they came back to finish me off! (*Laughs.*) You at least drink in front of her; I still don't have the nerve. It makes me furious with myself.

JAKE. The only way to win with them is to leave town.

MARILYN. You think so? Try Philadelphia. We could always kill them, I suppose.

JAKE. Short-range solutions.

MARILYN. You at least, they know you're alive!! No matter what I do you know how it feels? I'll put it this way: If *you* take them some place in your car, you're this wonderful success who can afford his own car; if I take them some place in my car, I'm the chauffeur. More than anything, you know what kills me? The thing I loved most was you and Mama in the kitchen with your stories. She'd tell one, you'd tell one, she'd tell one, you'd tell one. I thought someday I'll be old enough to have my own real experiences and then *I'll* have stories! To this day they will now allow me to tell a story. Isn't it crazy that I should still be bothered by that?

JAKE. I told my stories to get away from her stories.

MARILYN. Who gets away? How did we ever make it out of Queens in one piece?

JAKE. I got drafted out.

MARILYN. But how did I get out?

JAKE. What makes you think you're out?

MARILYN. You don't think so, huh? Maybe you're right. You think I'm that bad? I suppose I am.

JAKE. How often do you call them on the phone?

MARILYN. Who counts?

JAKE. Once a day?

MARILYN. At least.

JAKE. I don't speak to them more than once a week. When I get a message that they called I let a couple of days go by before I call back. How often do you have them over?

MARILYN. Half the time they invite themselves.

JAKE. With me they know better.

MARILYN. So do I.

JAKE. How often do you run down to Riverdale to do their shopping for them?

MARILYN. Cut it out, you're depressing me.

JAKE. Why can't they order by phone?

MARILYN. Mama says they hold you up if you order by phone. Who knows?

JAKE. Next time, simply refuse to go.

MARILYN. You are giving me a heart attack!

JAKE. You are a married woman with two kids and a well-paying job—

MARILYN. Not so well-paying.

JAKE. And you're too busy to run errands for them.

Now tell them. You can tell them. Tell them.

MARILYN. (*Shudders.*) You give me the creeps when
you talk like that. You sound like you hate them.
(*Pause.* JAKE *avoids a response.*) If you hate them so
much, why don't you break off entirely?

JAKE. Look, they are hardly the most important thing
going on in my life. Why overreact? They're old; a couple of phone calls keep them happy.

MARILYN. We used to be so close and now we see
things so differently. You were the one person in the
family I could go to for help.

JAKE. Who could I go to?

MARILYN. Me. (JAKE *turns away, no response.*
MARILYN *is hurt.* HE *pours drink.*) Boy! (JAKE, *noticing
effect on her, begins devouring tray of hors d'oeuvres.*)

JAKE. Christ, these are good. I don't know, Marilyn.
Louise! Jeez. Louise is so insanely loyal. This is a
wonderful story. I invited some *Times* colleagues over
for dinner. Not such a big deal, except that Louise hates
The New York Times (as much as *they* think it comes
down from Mount Sinai). O.K.? Because I report all my
fights, all this inter-office crap—you know, it's no different where you are—office politics, O.K.? But Louise
worked in an office for 15 minutes once when she was
on vacation from Mount Holyoke, so she doesn't
understand; she takes it personally. So I come home,
bitch, bitch, bitch, bitch, bitch, that's it, it's over, I
go to work happy the next morning. While Louise hates.
How can they do this to her Jake? Off with their heads!
O.K.? So when I invite my oppressors home to dinner,
she goes bananas. "How can you sit down at the same
table with these pigs? How can you eat with them?!"
Right? But finally she agrees. Grudgingly. You want to
know how grudgingly? This is a week ago Tuesday. I

come home; she's got a roast chicken in the oven, it smells marvelous. The apartment looks beautiful. I check out the dining room. There are only four chairs. We're having eight to dinner. I say, "Louise, what happened to the chairs?" "They are being repaired," she says. "They broke this morning and I sent them out to be repaired." Possibly a little hostile. O.K.? We call her brother, Mickey. Mickey's her Mr. Fix-it. Lives three blocks away. Comes running over with four chairs. Fine. We get through the dinner. Louise won't talk to anybody, but no problem: My colleagues talk to much to notice wives not talking. Bruce Forrester is charming, Glen Applebaum is charming, *The New York Times* voltage meter on charm, way up there. Louise hates them all. "Establishment assholes," she calls them. A ten-minute shit-fit after they leave. I'm a sell-out, a hypocrite, she can't talk to me any more. She calls her brother, Mickey; she wants to go over. Mickey says, "It's midnight." "It's irrelevant," says Louise, "I'm coming over." Mickey says, "Fine, bring the chairs." So, at 12:30, Louise and I are struggling up West End Avenue with four chairs. Louise is wheezing! I'm so pissed, I can't see straight. We get up to Broadway. She goes on strike. She sits down on a chair (JACK *enters from garden, stands by door and listens.* JAKE *includes him in his audience.*) What am I supposed to do? I sit down on a chair. People start coming out of the subway; they see us, they make cracks. It's very strange to see two grown people sitting on chairs outside the subway on Broadway at 12:30 in the morning. I feel like a total ass, but Louise loves it. She cracks back at the people coming out the the subway, and soon there's a small crowd gathered around us. My wife is a hell of a better hostess on the street than at her own dinner party. Three street musicians show up—they play. Why not? There's always music on the Johnny Carson show. Here's Louise! In the end, Louise talks four guys in the crowd to carry the chairs over to Mickey's for us.

MARILYN. God, that Louise is a scream, Jake. You know that?

JACK. I missed it. Jake?

JAKE. You heard it.

JACK. I came in late.

JAKE. You heard most of it, Dad.

JACK. Most of it leaves some out. Who knows what I heard?

JAKE. Well, I can't tell it again.

MARILYN. Daddy, it's a wonderful story.

JAKE. I'm exhausted.

MARILYN. O.K., I'll tell it. Listen to this. Last week Jake and Louise had a dinner party last week for some people on the *Times*—

JACK. Big shots. He invites the big shots.

JAKE. No big shots.

JACK. Don't tell me.

MARILYN. Well, Louise has a thing against the *Times*—

JACK. No, she doesn't.

MARILYN. Yeah, you see? Whenever Jake comes home with, you know a story about his rotten day at the office, Louise identifies. Not only does she get mad, she stays mad. But Jake's not mad—

JAKE. No, I'm not mad. (JAKE *grins, continues to grin as* HE *listens to story.*)

MARILYN. But Louise has conniption fits. So by this time Jake is long over being mad. Jake invites these colleagues of his home for dinner, and Louise—she can't stand to have them in her house. You understand?

JACK. That's awful. That's terrible. Go on. Go on.

MARILYN. So here's Jake, he's hosting this big dinner party, and he comes home and Louise is cooking away in the kitchen. Cooking, cooking, cooking. Everything is peachy-keen, except when he goes in the dining room, you know, something is very, very wrong.

JACK. What?

MARILYN. There are eight people for dinner—right? And there are only four chairs. Four chairs! Can you believe it?! (HELEN *enters.* JAKE *loses his grin.*)

HELEN. (*With* MARILYN.) Can you believe that gang? Eat you out of house and home.

MARILYN. That day Louise sent them out to be repaired! Look who's here. (JACK *begins scratching his hand.* JAKE *pours drink.*) Where was I? Yeah. So what are they going to do about these chairs? Because Louise sent them out that day, you know, to be repaired, and they didn't—I guess they didn't come back in time—they were—Were they supposed to come back that day and they didn't, Jake, or what?

JAKE. It's not important.

MARILYN. What? This is unconscious or conscious on her part? What motivates her behavior?

JAKE. Maybe I'd better tell this.

MARILYN. Hold your horses! So anyway, they go out—No, they don't. Yes, they do. Jake and Louise, to get some chairs. What—you left Edie alone?

JAKE. She was asleep.

MARILYN. So early?

JAKE. This is after dinner, Marilyn, not before.

MARILYN. O.K., so I'm a little mixed up. What's the difference? It's no big deal, it's a lousy story. Mama, they get the chairs and they have the dinner and everybody has a terrible time—

JAKE. No.

MARILYN. Everybody has a good time, and they go home, and Jake and Louise wait till Edie's asleep and then they take back the chairs. Did I get it right that time? (JAKE *nods*.) And they're on the street, you know, with these stupid chairs, and it's like two in the morning, um, and what happens is very funny and I don't remember what it is, and anyway I'd screw it up.

JACK. Marilyn . . . Marilyn . . . Where were they going with the chairs?

MARILYN. Back to Mickey's. You know!

HELEN. Her brother?

JAKE. Right. Yeah, right.

MARILYN. I left that out?

JACK. Mickey was there for dinner?

MARILYN. (*To* JAKE.) Was Mickey there for dinner?

JAKE. Mickey was not there for dinner.

MARILYN. You don't have to snap at me.

JAKE. I didn't snap.

HELEN. So all these famous people were at your house, Jake?

JAKE. No, Ma, just friends.

HELEN. Some friends from work?

JAKE. That's right.

HELEN. From *The New York Times*?

JAKE. That's right.

HELEN. It must have been a very scintillating evening.

JAKE. Not during dinner.

HELEN. After dinner?

JAKE. After the guests left.

HELEN. You're pulling your Ma's leg, Jakey-boy?

JAKE. Look, I'll put it this way: Louise hates the *Times*, she hates everything about the *Times*, she would love me to work on the *Washington Post*.

JACK. Sure. Out of town.

JAKE. But when I ask my colleagues to dinner, well, she's really a loyal girl — O.K.? She grits her teeth and prepares this fabulous menu.

HELEN. You're going too fast for me, Jake. What did you serve?

JAKE. Roast chicken basted in butter.

HELEN. Mmm.

JAKE. Corn on the cob and brussel sprouts.

HELEN. My mouth is watering.

JAKE. And the apartment — O.K.? — it's — well, Ma, even you would think she did a good job. How can I describe it? A show place, Ma.

HELEN. Radio City?

JAKE. Better, Ma. The Taj Mahal. But, Ma, I go into the dining room — are you listening? — and the dining room table is set for a banquet, a royal banquet. Our best sterling silver, tall elegant glasses — they sparkle, our best china, Ma, the plates shine! But there's one problem —

HELEN. Didn't I know it.

JAKE. We are eight for dinner. Eight — O.K.? But there are four chairs at the table.

HELEN. Ah-ha! A riddle! Your Ma loves riddles. What happened to the other four chairs?

JACK. Yeah, Jake, yeah! (ALL *look at* JAKE *in wonder.*)

MARILYN. This you gotta hear!

JAKE. Well! . . . (*About to continue story.*)

CURTAIN

ACT TWO

TIME: *One year later.* JAKE *and* LOUISE'S *apartment on West End Avenue, the living room. Not unattractive, but absent-mindedly furnished; nothing quite works together. An archway leads to the hall,* EDIE'S *bedroom, door closed and the front door.* JAKE'S *desk is hemmed into a corner, out of place, littered with page proofs. At rise,* JAKE *is seated, turned away from the desk, anxiously facing* LOUISE, *who is on the telephone.* LOUISE *is in her 30's, extremely attractive.*

LOUISE. It's nice to hear your voice, too, Jack . . . You sound so much stronger . . . Well, you gave us a worry . . . No, nothing especially . . . You know, her usual adorable self . . . Well, she misses you too . . . Well, we'll make up for it on Sunday . . . Of course, it's still on . . . Now, Jack . . . now, no one thinks that . . . well, if Jake hasn't called you back I don't know, he must be — (*Flails at* JAKE *to come up with an excuse for why* HE *hasn't called his* FATHER *back.*) Oh, I do know, I forgot to tell him you called. I apologize, Jack. So, you see it's my fault. I usually have a memo pad right here by the phone so I can take messages, but I don't know what's become of it . . . Well, if you bought me a new one I'd love it because it's a present from you . . . (*Flails at* JAKE *as if to ask "How do I get off?"*) Well, I'm sure he's all right, Jack. It isn't all hours of the night, now don't exaggerate, it's only 8:30 now . . . Not exactly. First he was going to Random House to pick up some galleys on his book and then he had a story or something to cover for the *Times* . . . Jack, don't even think that. He hasn't changed. You don't realize how busy he is. He's the same old Jake as ever, I promise you. (JAKE *mimes his head exploding.*) Well, I'll let Jake save that for you for Sunday . . . Oh, a whole lot, Jack. Yes, a whole lot is new, but Jake hates it when I tell you. (JAKE *mimes a groan and a collapse.*) She's inside doing her homework . . . Of course she's not too busy to say hello. (*Shouts.*) Edie! (*Pause.*) Edie! Pick up the phone in our room! Grandpa wants to say hello!

EDIE. (*Enters from bedroom.* SHE *is nine.*) Grandpa Jack or Grandpa Sam?

LOUISE. Grandpa Jack! Pick up the phone, Edie. (*To* JACK.) She's picking up Jack. One minute. (*Pause.*) So then, we'll see you on Sunday . . . I'm really looking forward to it. (*Covers phone with hand. Shouts.*) Edie! Pick up! (*To* JACK.) She was in the bathroom, Jack. (*Covers phone. To* JAKE.) Will you see what's keeping that child? (*Into phone.*) I'm sorry Helen isn't feeling well. Are you sure she'll be all right for Sunday? Because we can always — Well, tell her I said to take is easy. But the most important thing is her health. And your health. (*To* JAKE.) Jake! Do something, goddammit, or I'll tell him you're here! (JAKE *leaves room.*) She'll be there in a second, Jack. Any second.

EDIE. (*Offstage.*) (*To* JAKE.) I'm picking up.

LOUISE. See? (JAKE *returns, nodding his head.* LOUISE *covers phone. To* JAKE.) She's picked up.

JAKE. I know. (*He sits at his desk, staring at* LOUISE *on telephone.* LOUISE *listens, then nods to* JAKE *that everything is fine. Another long moment passes as* JAKE *fidgets at his desk and* LOUISE *fidgets on the phone.*)

LOUISE. She really has to finish her homework now, Jack . . . Yes, you do, Edie. Fine, Jack. Me too. Me too

. . . Hang up now, Edie . . . I know it . . . she is, isn't she? . . . Yes, she really is. Yes, she is. I don't know where she gets it . . . That's true . . . She is . . . You couldn't be more right about it. She is . . . If he doesn't get in too late. And this time I promise I won't forget to tell him. You have my word. (*Laughs.*) Now, Jack, is that nice? I thought you were my friend. (*Laughs.*) So do I. (*Laughs.*) So do I. (*Laughs.*) Absolutely. (*Laughs.*) I can't wait. My love to Helen. (*Hangs up. To* JAKE.) They're coming. The parents are coming! (*Runs about.*) The parents are coming! The parents are coming! To arms! To arms! (JAKE *laughs, rises, embraces her.*) They make you so tense, poor Jake. I don't make you take calls from my mother, do I? Do I? Shh. I'm joking. Shall we hide? Shall we leave town?

JAKE. They're really coming Sunday. Shit. (*Parts from embrace.*)

LOUISE. All we talked about in the hospital was his granddaughter, poor man.

JAKE. His granddaughter and his son, the journalist. Thank God I work at the *Times* or he'd have trouble remembering my name.

LOUISE. My mother calls me Mickey three-fifths of the time. Jack is dear, but if Helen criticized my house again—she hates my taste—I'll poison her.

JAKE. My mother? You think she'll notice? The worst cook in the world.

LOUISE. Next to me.

JAKE. Close. I know what you can do. She mostly notices furniture. Get rid of the chairs again.

LOUISE. I should. Wouldn't it be wonderful, Jake, if I got rid of all the furniture? They arrive here on Sunday and Helen traipses in—you know the way she does—as if she buys the place—and there's not a stitch here. No furniture. No rugs. No pictures. "Oh Louise, what a veritable place! I can't believe what you've done to this place."

JAKE. (*Laughs.*) That's right. That's right.

LOUISE. (*Crosses to wall, gestures.*) "Oh Louise, I just love this part of the wall. (*Crosses c., points to floor.*) And the floor. What have you done to the floor?"

JAKE. "My! My! Is that a floor or is that a floor?"

LOUISE. "It is such a tidy floor. (*Looks to ceiling. In wonder:*) And the ceiling! Jack, have you ever seen such a ceiling?"

JAKE. (*As JACK.*) "What's new, son? Where's my granddaughter? (*Squawks like a parrot.*) What's new? Where's my granddaughter? What's new? Where's my granddaughter? What's new? What's new? What's new? (*Sobering.*) Nu? Nu? Nu? Nu? Nu? Nu?" (*Works his way back to desk, sits, shuffles proofs.*)

LOUISE. "Louise, what a perfectly perfect crack in the wall, what a gorgeous piece of dust in the corner. Will you look, Jack? See all the dust Louise is collecting? Why, Louise, you must let me take this dust home and knit you a sweater."

JAKE. Baby, I better get down to work or else . . .

LOUISE. She lies like a glove, your mother.

JAKE. Take it easy, will you? She hasn't had such an easy life. And the phrase is rug. Not glove. She lies like a rug.

LOUISE. Yes. She lies like a rug. (*Crosses to his chair, stands there. Pause.*) Oh, it'll be fine, Jake.

JAKE. (*Studying proof.*) Didn't you have something to read?

LOUISE. Miss Marple. (*Continues to stare down at him.*)

JAKE. (*After a pause.*) What?

LOUISE. I'm sorry. (*Retreats to her chair, picks up paperback, reads as* JAKE *works.*) I know who did it.

JAKE. No you don't.

LOUISE. It's the vicar, isn't it? (*No response.*) Jake, isn't it the vicar? (*No response.*) I have to know! (*No response.*) I'm going to look.

JAKE. (*Turns to her.*) You are not.

LOUISE. I have to know.

JAKE. You will know when you finish the book.

LOUISE. What do you care if I look?

JAKE. Then why bother? Why read it in the first place? If you don't intend to do it right, why do it at all? Go ahead, look. I don't give a damn. You never intended to read it anyway.

LOUISE. It's only a murder mystery, for Christ's sake! (*JAKE, annoyed, turns back to his work.*) I won't look. (*Stares at* JAKE *working.*) Jake, I won't look! (*Pause.*) What a thing to get mad about. I said I wouldn't look. (*Waits for a response. There is none.*) You stink! (*Goes back to her reading.*)

EDIE. (*Offstage.*) Mommy! (LOUISE *doesn't answer, continues reading.*) Mommy! (JAKE *looks up from his proofs and over at* LOUISE, *waiting for her to answer her* CHILD's *call.*) Mommy! I need you! (LOUISE *continues to read.* JAKE *continues to stare at* LOUISE, *then goes back to his work.*)

LOUISE. Shit, it's not the vicar. (*Turns page. Long silence as* LOUSIE *reads,* JAKE *works.*)

EDIE. (*Offstage.*) Daddy!

JAKE. (*Very quickly.*) What is it, angel?

EDIE. (*Offstage.*) Can you come here, please?

JAKE. I'm working, honey!

EDIE. Daddy, please!

JAKE. What is it?

EDIE. I need you! (JAKE *puts down his work, glares at* LOUISE, *who does not look up, and enters* EDIE'S *bedroom.*)

JAKE. I'm working, honey.

EDIE. I'm sorry.

JAKE. What is it?

EDIE. What's the capital of Rumania?

JAKE. Edie, I think that's something you should look up for yourself.

EDIE. I can't.

JAKE. Yes, you can.

EDIE. I don't have time.

JAKE. In the time we're talking about it you could have looked it up.

EDIE. In the time we're talking about it you could have told me.

JAKE. You should learn to learn things on your own.

EDIE. Daddy, I promise. Only tell me this time.

JAKE. Bucharest.

EDIE. Spell it.

JAKE. B-U-C-H-A-R-E-S-T. That's the last time I do that for you.

EDIE. Thank you, Daddy.

JAKE. Anything else? (*No answer.*) Do you have a lot more homework?

EDIE. I don't know.

JAKE. What do you mean you don't know?

EDIE. I don't know how much it is until I do it.

JAKE. I'm going back to work now.

EDIE. Thanks, Dad. (JAKE *exits bedroom, takes his seat at desk, goes back to work. Stops, turns to* LOUISE.)

JAKE. I think we should talk about something.

LOUISE. (*Reading.*) Must we?

JAKE. We must.

LOUISE. Can it wait?

JAKE. Baby, please put down that book.

LOUISE. (*Goes on reading for a few seconds then, with effort, drags her eyes off the page and up to* JAKE.) I'm in the middle of this.

JAKE. I want to bring to your attention something you do that bears discussion. Then you can go back to your book.

LOUISE. Can it wait five minutes, then I'll be through with this chapter.

JAKE. (*After a pause.*) O.K. (*She goes to her book,* HE *to his work. But* HE *can't work.* HE *fidgets, shuffles papers, finally turns, stares at her as* SHE *reads.* LOUISE *eventually becomes aware of the stare and looks up at him.* SHE *closes her book and puts it on the end table.*) Do you do it on purpose or what?

LOUISE. Do what on purpose?

JAKE. She called you three or four times and you didn't answer.

LOUISE. Oh, is that what you're upset about?

JAKE. You acted as if you didn't hear her.

LOUISE. I didn't.

JAKE. You had to.

LOUISE. But I didn't. I was concentrating on Agatha Christie.

JAKE. And I was concentrating on these proofs. But I heard her.

LOUISE. O.K., so I didn't hear her. So why are you getting so mad about it?

JAKE. I'm mad because you don't even know it's a problem.

LOUISE. What's a problem? Oh, really, Jake!

JAKE. You don't know how many times a day I witness this. I should have brought it up before.

LOUISE. That I don't hear her? That's not true. I always hear her.

JAKE. Not this time.

LOUISE. When it's important I hear her.

JAKE. How do you know whether it's important?

LOUISE. I know.

JAKE. Look, I don't care if it's important or not, when a kid calls its mother the mother should answer.

LOUISE. Now I'm a bad mother.

JAKE. I didn't say that.

LOUISE. It's in your stare.

JAKE. Is that another thing you know? My stare?

LOUISE. I'm sorry if I'm a bad mother.

JAKE. You're not a bad mother. But you shouldn't make the child feel she's ignored.

LOUISE. You're not with her all day.

JAKE. Neither are you if you ignore her.

LOUISE. I don't ignore her. My mind was on my book. You're the one who gave it to me!

JAKE. I want you to read.

LOUISE. I can't do two things at the same time.

JAKE. You can't read and listen?

LOUISE. If I'm involved I can't.

JAKE. That's the most ridiculous statement I've ever heard of. What if the house caught fire? You mean if you were reading you wouldn't smell smoke? If a bomb fell and you were reading you'd just go on reading?

LOUISE. Oh, all right, you don't want me to read so I won't read.

JAKE. I do want you to read. You stopped reading two years ago and I've been trying to get you back to it ever since. And you know it.

LOUISE. O.K. then. (*Starts to pick up her book.*)

JAKE. That's why I gave you Agatha Christie.

LOUISE. Jake —

JAKE. All you did for two years was lie around—

LOUISE. I was in a depression.

JAKE. and stare into space.

LOUISE. You know I was in a depression.

JAKE. I'm in a depression right now. And I still read!

LOUISE. I'm my own person.

JAKE. Who doesn't read.

LOUISE. I have my own life.

JAKE. You have made that perfectly clear. Any number of times.

LOUISE. Get a new wife!

JAKE. Louise—

LOUISE. If I'm such a terrible mother, do you want a divorce?

JAKE. I do not think you're a terrible mother and no, thank you, I do not want a divorce. Why is it that whenever I bring up any difference between us you ask me if I want a divorce?

LOUISE. You don't have to stay with me if you don't want to.

JAKE. You always do this!

LOUISE. I can't help what I am.

JAKE. Yes, you can.

LOUISE. Well, if I can, why don't you? Why am I the only one who has to change!

JAKE. I try! I haven't had a drink in four months.

LOUISE. You're disgusting when you drink.

JAKE. A cigarette in a year. Sure you can help what you are. I'm a lot different from when you met me. You say it all the time.

LOUISE. Oh, you're not always different.

JAKE. Now, suddenly, I'm not different. You use any argument that's convenient.

LOUISE. You have a way of talking to me that makes me feel like a criminal.

JAKE. To you any criticism is a death blow. I tell you we don't have any butter in the house, you ask me if I want a divorce. Why is it you can only react in extremes? I have brought up one thing that you do with Edie that I don't think you notice that I have noticed for some time but which I have deliberately not brought up before because I had hoped you would notice it for yourself and stop doing it and also—frankly, baby, I have to say this—I knew if I brought it up we'd get into exactly the kind of circular argument we're in right now. And I wanted to avoid it. But I haven't and we're in it, so now, with your permission, I'd like to talk about it.

LOUISE. You don't see how that puts me down?

JAKE. What?

LOUISE. If you think I'm so stupid why do you go on living with me?

JAKE. *Dammit! Why can't anything ever be simple around here?!*

LOUISE. Oh, all right. Have it your way.

JAKE. I don't want it my way, I only want to talk about something you do with Edie. That's all!

LOUISE. That I ignore my child. Is that all?

JAKE. Don't you—Look—here's what I mean. O.K.? Here's another example. She came in before and I don't know what you were doing. You weren't reading.

LOUISE. Making your dinner.

JAKE. Didn't *you* eat dinner tonight? Wasn't it your dinner too?

LOUISE. I don't want to start a fight.

JAKE. Making my dinner. Jesus!

LOUISE. Well, I was. You just don't like to admit it.

JAKE. I admit it.

LOUISE. You say you do but you don't.

JAKE. Baby, you made my fucking dinner! Now can we get back to what we were talking about?

LOUISE. It's an old story. What do you want, Jake?

JAKE. Baby, what I want—I would like you to be more aware of what you do which you don't intend to be harmful or without feeling but which comes over, whether you know it or not, as without feeling.

LOUISE. Oh, now I don't love her. Is that it?

JAKE. My mother loves me too. She pulled the same shit.

LOUISE. Goddammit, I'm not your mother!

JAKE. Thank God for that!

LOUISE. You always compare me to your mother.

JAKE. No, I don't. I compare Edie to me. I remember what it was like to be a kid. And Edie is a lot like me—thank God, not in too many ways—but enough ways. And I know she's sensitive to a certain kind of behavior on your part which is similar to stuff my mother pulled on me.

LOUISE. All right, what do I *pull* on her, Jake. Tell me, what do I *pull?*

JAKE. What you pull is that you treat her as if she's not there.

LOUISE. She's always there. You're the one who's not there. She's there and I'm there. All day together. And you come home at night, drink your Tab and judge.

JAKE. We're not talking about what I do. We can talk about what I do later. Later I'll be more than happy to talk about what I do. But first, if it's possible, I would like to talk about what you do. Finally, if we can ever possibly manage it, that's the subject I would dearly love to get to.

LOUISE. I will not be talked to that way.

JAKE. Damn it! O.K. Look. This is doing neither of us any good.

LOUISE. You started it.

JAKE. Let me just say it. It'll take thirty seconds and it'll be over. I'll say what I want to. Without interruption. You say what you want to after I finish. And it'll be over and done with.

LOUISE. When you put it that way, O.K. Go ahead.

JAKE. Was my tone of voice acceptable that time?

LOUISE. Screw you!

JAKE. O.K. I admit I did it that time. That time, I know I did it. I couldn't resist. I'm sorry.

LOUISE. You can never resist.

JAKE. Sometimes you ask for it.

LOUISE. You talk about what I do to Edie, what do you think you do to me?

JAKE. This is not the time to go into what we each do to each other.

LOUISE. So I'm a terrible wife too. A terrible wife and a terrible mother. I really don't see why you don't leave me.

JAKE. I swear to God—

LOUISE. O.K. Say what this terrible thing is I did.

JAKE. Edie comes into the kitchen. I realize you were busy. I do appreciate that. Seriously.

LOUISE. O.K.

JAKE. And she asked you five times if she could stay up late to watch *Three's Company*.

LOUISE. It wasn't five times

JAKE. And you never—You didn't answer.

LOUISE. It wasn't five times, Jake. Don't exaggerate.

JAKE. Three times?

LOUISE. Twice. If it was even that much.

JAKE. Why didn't you answer?

LOUISE. I don't know why. My mind was on my cooking. What do I care what she watches?

JAKE. Don't you see how that makes her feel?

LOUISE. Let her stay up to watch it. Is that what you want?

JAKE. Staying up late is not the issue.

LOUISE. Then she doesn't get enough sleep and I can't get her up for school in the morning. You get her up for school sometime!

JAKE. That's not the point!

LOUISE. It's *my* point.

JAKE. It's hopeless!

LOUISE. Then get a divorce.

JAKE. I don't want—

LOUISE. I do listen to her. Where were you when she broke her leg?

JAKE. At work.

LOUISE. Who calmed her down? Who took her to the hospital? Who stayed with her?

JAKE. I'm not denying that you're good in emergencies.

LOUISE. *You* panicked!

JAKE. I don't deny you react better than I do in emergencies. I am terrible in emergencies. I grant you that. But the point is—

LOUISE. Your point, not mine.

JAKE. *My* point is that there is more to raising a child than being good in emergencies. Being good when there are no emergencies is equally important. My mother always used to tell me, "Don't trust your friends. Only your family will be there when you need them." And I used to tell her, "I also want people there when I don't need them. That's just as important."

LOUISE. I'm not your mother!

JAKE. It's analogous. Do you want another example?

LOUISE. I can give examples too, you know!

JAKE. Not of that!

LOUISE. Of other things!

JAKE. Fine. But not when we're talking about this.

LOUISE. O.K. We talked about it. I still don't see what I do that's so bad.

JAKE. You act as if she's not there!

LOUISE. You refused to do her diapers!

JAKE. Christ! Nine years ago!

LOUISE. So don't tell me I'm not there. Who changed her?

JAKE. It was your job.

LOUISE. Other fathers do it.

JAKE. I'm not other fathers!

LOUISE. I'm not other mothers!

JAKE. Fine!

LOUISE. So get a divorce.

JAKE. You know what's the—

EDIE. (*Offstage.*) Daddy!

JAKE. I can't now, Edie!

EDIE. I need you!

JAKE. I can't! I'm working!

EDIE. What on?

JAKE. My book!

EDIE. Just for a minute.

LOUISE. You spoil her. She has your number.

JAKE. I *what*?

EDIE. Daddy!

LOUISE. Spoil her. She's Daddy's girl. She twists you around her finger.

JAKE. Bullshit! (HE *goes to* EDIE.) Edie, you've got to stop bothering me when I'm working. I have a deadline. (*While* JAKE *is in with* EDIE, LOUISE *sits fuming.* SHE *picks up her paperback and hurls it across the room.* SHE *mutters, "Now see what you made me do."* SHE *gets up to retrieve it. "Bastard."* SHE *picks it up and the bind-*

ing comes loose. The pages fall out. "Dirty bastard."
SHE *drops to her knees to put the pages in order.*)

EDIE. You weren't working. I heard you talking.

JAKE. I was talking to Mommy.

EDIE. What were you talking about?

JAKE. That doesn't concern you.

EDIE. Were you fighting?

JAKE. If we were fighting it doesn't concern you. People fight all the time. It doesn't mean anything. Don't be afraid when people fight.

EDIE. What's the capital of Philadelphia?

JAKE. Philadelphia is a city.

EDIE. So what's the capital?

JAKE. It doesn't have a capital.

EDIE. Yes, it does.

JAKE. No, it doesn't. States have capitals.

EDIE. So what's Washington? Isn't that a capital?

JAKE. Washington is the capital of the United States.

EDIE. And it's a city.

JAKE. It's a District.

EDIE. It's a city.

JAKE. It's a district. The District of Columbia. That's what they call it.

EDIE. I don't get it.

JAKE. It's too complicated to explain tonight. Edie, you have to figure some of these things out for yourself. You've got the Book of Knowledge there. Philadelphia is the capital of the state of Pennsylvania. Or is it Harrisburg?

EDIE. I think that's wrong.

JAKE. Look it up.

EDIE. I don't have time.

JAKE. Now don't call me again.

EDIE. You don't want to help me. (JAKE *exits,*

discovers LOUISE *on her knees retrieving and lining up pages of her paperback.*)

LOUISE. Why don't you ever make her come to you?

JAKE. What's the difference?

LOUISE. The difference is discipline.

JAKE. Bullshit!

LOUISE. The difference is that you're the adult and she's the child.

JAKE. I don't believe in that authority crap. I had that up to here!

LOUISE. That's why it's so hard for me.

JAKE. I make it hard for you, I suppose.

LOUISE. You make me the bad one.

JAKE. What happened to the book?

LOUISE. I come out the villian.

JAKE. That was a new book. Look at it already! Hitler didn't do to books what you do!

LOUISE. She calls "Daddy" and you come running. I don't come running so that makes me Hitler. Now who talks in extremes?

JAKE. A little respect for the printed word —

LOUISE. Why don't you ever make her come to see you? Why do you always go to her?

JAKE. You want me to play power games with a nine year old? I want her to know I'm interested in her. Someone around here has to show interest in her.

LOUISE. You love her more than I do.

JAKE. I didn't say that.

LOUISE. Yes, you did.

JAKE. You don't know how to listen. You have never learned how to listen. It's as if listening to you is a foreign language.

LOUISE. I try to drill some responsibility in her during the day and you come home at night and undo everything. No wonder she has no respect for me.

JAKE. I'm not going to listen to this!

LOUISE. I liked you better when you were drinking. You didn't undermine me.

JAKE. You want me to have a drink?

LOUISE. When you were drinking you were only mean when you were drunk. But *now!*

JAKE. O.K. I get it. You want me to go back on the booze.

LOUISE. You do exactly what you want to do. You always have and you always will.

JAKE. O.K.! If that's what you want! (*Goes to bar.*) Can I make you something?

LOUISE. I swear, Jake, if you make yourself a drink I'll leave you.

JAKE. (*Puts down bottle.*) What the fuck is going on inside that head of yours? Is that a sane reaction? If I take a drink—one drink—you'll leave me? I ask you: is that sane?

LOUISE. I mean it!

JAKE. Go fuck yourself!

LOUISE. Fuck you right back!

JAKE. Fuck you, yourself! Don't you realize you have a child inside? What's the matter with you? I really think you're crazy! (LOUISE *breaks down into tears.*) Terrific. (JAKE *crosses to her.*) I'm not going to have a drink. I didn't even want one.

LOUISE. Why do you do this to me?

JAKE. I don't do a goddammed thing.

LOUISE. I think maybe we should separate.

JAKE. We are not going to separate.

LOUISE. I can't take anymore. I want to die.

JAKE. You don't want to die.

LOUISE. I do.

JAKE. You have responsibilities.

LOUISE. I don't care!

JAKE. You really want to die? Go ahead and die! But just remember one thing. I can die too. I can die just as fast as you.

LOUISE. Don't talk to me that way.

JAKE. You want to see me die? I don't have to just threaten it, I'm quite capable of doing it. You want to see me go through that window right now?

LOUISE. Jake, do you know how scared you make me when you talk this way?

JAKE. Just remember what happens to children of suicides. They often commit suicide too. So it's not just you who dies — oh no — you've also murdered your child. Is that what you want? Hemingway's father committed suicide! Look, neither one of us is going to die. I'm not going to have a drink. I love you . . . O.K.?

LOUISE. I do love you. I know you're going to leave me someday.

JAKE. You always say that! You're the only person in my entire life I've ever been able to make a commitment to. It makes me furious when you say I'm going to leave you. How could I leave you? This thing is not going to fail. I want this thing to work! Don't you want it to work? (*A pause.* THEY *are about to reach out for each other.*)

EDIE. (*Offstage.*) Daddy!

LOUISE. Don't go.

EDIE. (*Offstage.*) Daddy, I need you!

LOUISE. Don't go, Jake.

JAKE. You come here, angel!

EDIE. I can't!

JAKE. Yes, you can!

EDIE. I'm busy.

LOUISE. Don't give in to her!

JAKE. I'm busy too.

EDIE. You're only talking.

JAKE. I'm not coming there, you come here. (*Long pause. No response.*)

LOUISE. She has your number.

JAKE. I didn't go, did I?

LOUISE. Look at you, you're a nervous wreck.

JAKE. I'm a nervous wreck because of our fight, not Edie!

LOUISE. Yes! I don't have half the power over you she has.

JAKE. Power. Power. Do you actually want power over me, Louise?

LOUISE. You're terrified of your own daughter.

JAKE. Christ! I will go in to her if you keep up with that. You'll drive me to do the very thing you don't want me to do.

LOUISE. That's right. You'll go in there and then blame me.

EDIE. (*Offstage.*) Daddy! (JAKE *goes.*)

LOUISE. Perfect!

(*Throughout* JAKE *and* EDIE's *dialogue* LOUISE *does the following: sits for a long time, then crosses to the window, stares out the window, sees her reflection in the window, puts a hand to her hair to straighten it out, stops herself, mutters, "Pig," makes faces at herself in the window, mutters, "Fascist. Fascist. Fascist." Crosses to the fruit bowl and attacks an apple furiously.*)

JAKE. This is the last time tonight I'm coming in here.

EDIE. Who was Franklin?

JAKE. Franklin who?

EDIE. I don't know. Franklin. Who was he?

JAKE. Franklin Roosevelt? Franklin Pierce? Franklin Pangborn? Franklin Sinatra?

EDIE. Why are you mad at me?

JAKE. I'm not mad. What do you have to know for?

EDIE. I didn't do anything.

JAKE. I mean about Franklin. Look, Edie, there's a lot on Daddy's mind. This is the last time I'm coming in here tonight. Anyhow, it's way past your bedtime.

EDIE. I want to watch *Three's Company*.

JAKE. You can't watch anything until you finish your homework. Anyhow, *Three's Company* is half over.

EDIE. Why didn't anybody tell me!?

JAKE. Nobody's supposed to tell you! If you want to watch *Three's Company* you have to know when it's on for yourself.

EDIE. I don't have a *TV Guide*.

JAKE. It's in the newspaper.

EDIE. How am I supposed to find it in a whole newspaper?

JAKE. You *look*!

EDIE. I don't have time. I'm doing my homework. You want me to flunk out?

JAKE. Then you don't have time to watch *Three's Company*.

EDIE. This is my last question. If I finish this, can I watch the rest of *Three's Company*?

JAKE. If you get undressed at the same time. And into your pajamas and brush your teeth.

EDIE. Can I brush my teeth during the commercial?

JAKE. I don't care what you do as long as you are in bed with the lights out by the time *Three's Company* is over.

LOUISE. (*Shouts.*) And has her room straightened out!

EDIE. I'll be up all night!

JAKE. Do you promise to straighten it up tomorrow?

LOUISE. Not tomorrow. Tonight!

EDIE. It's unfair.

JAKE. You heard your mother.

EDIE. I can't do it all.

JAKE. Do as much as you can.

EDIE. I'll do as much as I can and I'll do the rest tomorrow.

JAKE. That's fine, fine.

EDIE. He has to do with the Constitutional Convention in Philadelphia.

JAKE. Benjamin Franklin.

EDIE. Oh yeah. I remember now. Thanks, Dad. (JAKE *returns to living room.*)

JAKE. You are never to do that again!

LOUISE. She wraps you around her little finger.

JAKE. When I tell her something you are not to countermand me!

LOUISE. I'm her mother!

JAKE. I'm her father!

LOUISE. You don't act it. You act more like her lover! Her obsequious lover!

JAKE. Someone has to give her the affection you deny her.

LOUISE. Oh no, not that one!

JAKE. It's true! How often do you hug her?

LOUISE. How often do you hug me?

JAKE. That's not the point!

LOUISE. You say you love me but I do all the hugging. Isn't that the point?

JAKE. Like everything else you insist on affection strictly on your own terms.

LOUISE. I'll take any terms I can get!

EDIE. (*Offstage.*) Good night, Mommy! Good night, Daddy?

LOUISE. Good night, Edie.

JAKE. Good night, angel.

EDIE. Mommy, I almost finished cleaning my room. I'll finish in the morning.

LOUISE. Good, darling.

EDIE. I didn't watch *Three's Company.*

JAKE. Go to sleep now.

EDIE. I will. Good night.

LOUISE and JAKE. Good night.

JAKE. You shouldn't have had a child. You wanted a puppy, a cocker spaniel. That's what you really want.

LOUISE. I love her.

JAKE. The way you love me.

LOUISE. I do love you. I just know you'll leave me.

JAKE. Please. Not again.

LOUISE. I know what I know.

JAKE. You don't.

LOUISE. Oh yes, you think you're so perfect; well, you're not as good as you think.

JAKE. (*Scatters proofs.*) Stop! Stop! Stop! Stop! Stop! Stop! Stop!

LOUISE. (*Scared.*) O.K. I'll stop.

JAKE. I love you. Please stop.

LOUISE. Oh, Jake. I've stopped.

JAKE. I want to burn this fucking book.

LOUISE. It's a beautiful book. It's a beautiful book. I apologize, Jake. I've stopped.

JAKE. I don't know a goddamned thing.

LOUISE. Don't. Don't. You're wonderful. Don't.

JAKE. O.K.

LOUISE. Oh, Jake.

JAKE. No further. I've stopped.

LOUISE. I do love you. Do you know that?

JAKE. I know. I know. I'm sorry. I know. (SHE *comes toward him, arm out.*) Louise . . . (THEY *are about to embrace.*)

EDIE. (*Offstage.*) Mommy, Daddy, you're talking too loud, I can't sleep! (THEY *instantly freeze.*)

JAKE. (*A finger to his lips.*) Shhhh.

CURTAIN

ACT THREE

TIME: *The following Sunday.* JAKE *and* LOUISE'S
apartment, spruced up for a party. At rise, LOUISE
*comes rushing out from bedroom fixing her hair,
crosses to couch, fluffs cushions.* EDIE *wanders out
from her bedroom.*

EDIE. Mommy!

LOUISE. You look lovely, darling. (*Impulsively hugs
her.*)

EDIE. I'm getting a headache. (LOUISE *releases* EDIE
as JAKE *enters.* LOUISE *turns away.*)

JAKE. (*Putting on jacket. To* EDIE.) You look good
enough to eat. (*Ignores* LOUISE, *who glares at him.
Doorbell chimes.*) Thank God! (*Heads for door.*)

LOUISE. Remember. We agreed. (JAKE *stops in his
tracks, turns on her coldly, then turns back to open
door. Standing in hall are* JACK, HELEN *and* MARILYN,
dressed for winter. THEY *enter.*)

JAKE. About time!

JACK. Where's my granddaughter?!

HELEN. Hello, Sonny, where's Louise? It's been so
long I forget—I have to go to the bathroom.

LOUISE. Helen, Jack! Marilyn, how good to see you
all!

HELEN. Louise, you look wonderful, I don't have
time to talk now, the place, you've done wonders, those
trees—The bathroom.

EDIE. Hi, Grandma!

HELEN. Darling! Isn't she—? (*Looking around.*)
Where—?

Louise. I'll show you, Helen. That's a lovely suit.

Helen. You like it? (They *exit.*)

Jack. Come to Grandpa, Edie!

Marilyn. (*Hands present to* Edie.) From Uncle Rudy and me.

Jake. (*Taking coats.*) Where's Rudy?

Marilyn. His turn to be sick.

Jake. Very original.

Marilyn. Maybe not original but he catches on quick.

Jake. (*To* Edie.) Say thank you.

Edie. I haven't opened it yet.

Marilyn. She doesn't know if she likes it, so why should she say thank you? Makes sense!

Jack. I'm going to squeeze the life out of you, do you hear? The very life! Where are you running? Give Grandpa a little squeeze. (Edie *giggles as* Jack *grabs her up in his arms.*)

Jake. No Rudy and no kids. This sounds dangerously close to fragmentation of the family, Marilyn.

Marilyn. Rudy took the kids out to Shelter Island for the weekend. What am I explaining for?

Jake. *I* always have to explain.

Marilyn. You have to explain because you're usually lying. But I'm telling the truth.

Jake. Ah, but when *you* tell the truth you feel like you're lying.

Marilyn. Very smart, my brother. Doesn't the chauffeur get offered a drink?

Jake. If you're driving, milk.

Marilyn. If you're not kidding, drop dead.

Edie. Your beard scratches, Grandpa!

Louise. Why is everyone standing at the door? Leaving so soon? Come in! Come in! Jake, do you mind getting the drinks? (Jake *starts off.*)

MARILYN. I'll supervise. (*Follows* JAKE *out.*) Not that I don't trust you.

LOUISE. (*Leading* JACK *into dining room.*) Jack, you'll strain yourself.

JACK. (*Releasing* EDIE.) I wouldn't know her, she's grown a foot!

EDIE. I'd know you!

JACK. You would? It's been so long how would you know me?

EDIE. Your beard scratches. That's one way. (JACK *and* LOUISE *laugh.*) And you always break my ribs. (BOTH *laugh.*)

JACK. She put the old man in his place, all right, all right. Do you want to come home tonight with Grandma and Grandpa, Edie?

EDIE. I have to go to school tomorrow.

JACK. Next weekend?

EDIE. I'll see.

JACK. "I'll see." What do you think of that? "I'll see." She's got such a vocabulary. She's certainly mature.

LOUISE. Sit down, Jack.

EDIE. Look, Mommy. (EDIE *displays* MARILYN'S *gift, a sweater.*)

LOUISE. Oh, Jack, that's lovely!

JACK. That's from Rudy and Jake, I mean Marilyn.

LOUISE. Where are Rudy and the children?

JACK. Rudy took the boys to Shelter Island. He works too hard, he deserves a little time off. What's the good word?

LOUISE. Oh, I was looking forward to a real old-fashioned family get-together. Jack, you look so handsome. Is that a new suit?

JACK. (*Proudly.*) Twenty-five years old.

LOUISE. I wish I could get Jake to pay as much attention to clothes as you do.

JACK. Jake? I had to dress him until he was twenty-one. Then he was too grown up to go shopping with his father.

LOUISE. You look wonderful. It's good to see you. You won't believe this, but you look younger than you did before you went into the hospital.

JACK. I get out of breath, it's the only change. Otherwise I feel like—

LOUISE. Well, Helen had better watch herself or some woman will start making eyes at you.

JACK. That's the silliest thing I ever heard of.

LOUISE. I honestly mean it. You don't know the kind of females out on the loose today.

JACK. Edie, when are you going to come home with Grandpa?

JAKE. (*Enters with* MARILYN.) What's new, Dad? What's the good word?

JACK. Louise was pulling the old man's leg.

LOUISE. No, I wasn't.

JAKE. No, she wasn't. Louise doesn't have a sense of humor.

LOUISE. Because I stop laughing at his stories after the hundreth time.

MARILYN. Ignore him, Louise. Have you redecorated?

LOUISE. That chair is new. (*Indicates.*)

EDIE. No, it's not, Mama. We got it last winter.

MARILYN. To me it's new. It looks so cheerful in here. I love your taste. Edie, do you like the sweater or do I take it back?

EDIE. I like it.

MARILYN. So what do you say?

EDIE. Thank you. (*Curtsies.*) Do I get to keep it now?

MARILYN. (*Laughs.*) The kid's a riot!

.

JACK. Edie, try the sweater on for Grandpa, Edie.

JAKE. Dad, what's new?

JACK. Not a thing. What's new with you?

JAKE. Not a thing. What's new?

JACK. What do you mean "not a thing"? What's new?

JAKE. Dad, I want to hear what's new. Now stop evading and tell me what's new!

JACK. (*To* LOUISE.) Do you know what he's talking about?

LOUISE. Jake, you're manic today.

JAKE. Ah! That's what's new!

JACK. So what do you have to say for yourself, young fellow?

HELEN. (*Enters with present.*) It's all so bright in here. You've built yourself a veritable Shangri-La, Louise. Who ever dreamed we'd find Shangri-La on West End Avenue, Dad?

JAKE. Hey, Ma, Dad doesn't want to tell me what's new.

JACK. (*Laughs.*) Son-of-a-gun! Don't think I'm not on to you. (EDIE *notices* HELEN'S *present, starts following her around.*)

JAKE. Nothing to drink, Dad?

JACK. I'm on the wagon.

JAKE. That makes two of us.

JACK. As I live and breathe!

JAKE. Sit down, Ma, what are you drinking? Scotch? A martini?

HELEN. You're flushed, Sonny, are you all right?

LOUISE. Won't you sit down, Helen? Can I get you anything?

HELEN. Louise, these plants! Talk about green thumbs! You must have a green arm! How do you keep the place clean? Oh, I almost forgot—

JACK. Edie's present!

HELEN. Dope that I am! I'm holding it in my hand and completely forgot about it. Where's that Edie? (ALL *laugh because* EDIE *is right behind her.* HELEN, *momentarily confused, turns and sees her.*) Can you beat it?! Look at us, gang, we're a vaudeville team. (EDIE *reaches for present.* HELEN *switches it from hand to hand as* EDIE *jumps for it,* BOTH *consciously putting on a show.*) A jumping jack! Can you beat it? (HELEN *finally relinquishes present.*) I surrender! (*To* OTHERS, *clasps her hands to bosom, sings.*) "I surrender, dear!" (*Scattered laughter as attention remains on* EDIE *tearing open her present.*) You'd think her life depended on it. (EDIE *gets the present unwrapped. It is* The Cat in the Hat *by Dr. Seuss.*)

EDIE. (*Dismayed.*) A book!

LOUISE. Let me see, darling. (EDIE *turns to* LOUISE *and shows book.*) She adores Dr. Seuss!

EDIE. I have this one.

LOUISE. You have so many. Are you sure?

EDIE. I've had it since I was a baby.

HELEN. The child who has everything.

JACK. We'll exchange it.

HELEN. You exchange it. I shopped like a dog for that book.

JACK. I'll exchange it.

HELEN. That'll be the day. You're not well enough to go shopping.

JACK. I can exchange a book.

HELEN. He can't walk downstairs without losing his breath.

EDIE. That's all right. I'll keep it.

HELEN. If you don't want it, don't keep it.

EDIE. That's all right.

HELEN. I never could get too many books. Come to Grandma, darling, look at the pictures with me.

EDIE. That's all right. I like it. Thank you, Grandma.

HELEN. Don't tell me you like it if you don't.

EDIE. No, I really like it. Thank you.

HELEN. You're not just saying it to make an old lady feel good?

EDIE. I really like it. I'm not lying.

HELEN. If you keep this one, when you come to our house to stay over, Grandma will take you to B. Dalton and you can buy any book you like. Give me a hug. (EDIE *hugs her.*) A real squeeze. That's more like it! You know, Edie, when I was a little girl you know what I dreamed of getting more than anything else? (*Pause.*)

LOUISE. Ask her what, darling.

EDIE. What?

HELEN. A library card. My very own library card. Because to me the library was this vast secret castle full of untold treasures. And the library card was the key. Do you have a library card?

EDIE. Somewhere.

HELEN. Show it to Grandma.

EDIE. I don't know where it is.

HELEN. Never lose your library card. It's one of your most valued possessions.

LOUISE. That's not always true, Helen. I spent more money on the library than I did on buying books.

HELEN. How did you manage that?

LOUISE. I was too lazy to take anything back. Oh, I kept books out for years! I finally owed so much they took away my card.

HELEN. A misspent youth. Jake, you never told me you married a juvenile delinquent.

LOUISE. I honestly was! I raided that library! I got

away with more books than when I had a card.

HELEN. That's not a very good lesson to teach your daughter.

LOUISE. Oh, Helen, don't you have any of the adventurer in you? The books I snitched—

JAKE. Snatched.

LOUISE. (*Ignores him.*)—are the ones I honestly cared about. My first Jane Austen was swiped from the library.

HELEN. I don't find this the least bit amusing.

LOUISE. Oh, come on, Helen, you must, buried deep within you, have a little larceny in your heart. Confess!

HELEN. Don't think I don't know the sort of fashionable thinking that goes today. I don't find it funny. And I don't think it's good conversation to have in front of children. Even in jest.

LOUISE. But, don't you see, Helen, that's where your ideas of child rearing differ from ours. Your generation hid things. We believe in being out in the open.

HELEN. (*To* JAKE.) What did I hide? I had so much to hide?

LOUISE. Oh, you know what I mean.

HELEN. I'm sorry to say you're way over my head.

LOUISE. Helen, I'm afraid you and I have a communications gap.

HELEN. (*To* JACK.) Do you know what she's talking about?

JAKE. Sounds to me like a vicious attack on libraries.

HELEN. It's gibberish to me.

JAKE. Mama is Honest Abe, Louise is Mack the Knife.

LOUISE. Mack the Knife. I like that!

JAKE. I take a middle position. I never went to the library. I assumed they wouldn't have what I wanted.

MARILYN. Denial is the spice of life.

JAKE. But I was never overdue.

MARILYN. You make a habit out of being overdue.

JAKE. But not at the library.

MARILYN. That I concede.

JAKE. At the library I'm clean. Aren't you proud of me, Mama?

HELEN. You're all out of my depth today. What's the matter with this gang?

JACK. (*To* EDIE.) Where are you going, darling?

EDIE. I want to count my books. (*Exits to bedroom.*)

JAKE. As long as we're on the subject of books—(*Crosses to desk, takes out proof of his book jacket. Hands it to* JACK.)

JACK. Is this it?

JAKE. That's only the jacket. Four hundred twenty-four pages go in between.

HELEN. What is it? Dad, let me see.

LOUISE. It's Jake's book.

HELEN. Already? Out already?

LOUISE. The pub date isn't for another three months, Helen.

HELEN. Pub date?

LOUISE. Publication date.

HELEN. You coulda fooled me, kid. I thought you meant a date to go drinking.

JACK. (*Studying jacket.*) Well, I'll be damned. Well, I'll be damned. Your name is almost as big as the title.

HELEN. Why not?

JACK. And this is the way they're going to let it look when it goes in the bookstores?

JAKE. Dad, that's the cover. A proof of the cover. That's exactly what it's going to look like.

JACK. You dirty son-of-a-gun! I ask you what's new and you hold out on me!

HELEN. (*Examining jacket.*) Jake, you'll be another

David Halberstam.

JAKE. He likes the book. He's giving me a quote.

HELEN. David Halberstam read your book?

JAKE. He's going to give me a quote.

HELEN. I'm so excited I can hardly breathe.

JACK. Well, I'll be damned! I'll be damned. You worked hard, Sonny boy, but it's paid off. Will you look at that book, Ma? (THEY *hold the jacket between them.*)

HELEN. It's a beautiful book.

JAKE. Galbraith is going to give me a quote.

JACK. You don't mean it!

HELEN. David Halberstam and John Kenneth Galbraith. Oh, Sonny, there are tears in my eyes. (*To* LOUISE.) When he was no older than six, Dad taught him to fold the *New York Times.* The coincidence! Who ever dreamed he'd be working for them? The patience it took. Jake wanted to fold it all at once. He couldn't wait. The mess he made of it. Dad showed him, no, you do it a little at a time, column by column until it gets folded. The concentration on his tiny face. I've often wondered if the patience to write a book isn't rooted in that childhood lesson.

JACK. Don't be silly.

HELEN. It's not such a crazy idea. The book I could write, I could teach you all a thing or two. And it wouldn't be about the world's business. I wouldn't have to go outside my own home. Now it can be told! What do you think of that, Jake? Your ma, a writerkeh? (*Dopey voice.*) And I wouldn't want no help neither. (*To* LOUISE.) Jake would never take any help. One of Dad's best customers is a printer on the *Times.* But Jake wouldn't let us ask him to get him a job. You always had to do everything yourself, Jake.

JAKE. I bet you could write a best seller, Ma.

HELEN. Don't laugh. I could yet.

MARILYN. How come nobody ever gave me a chance to turn down contacts?

HELEN. The old lady still has a few tricks in her.

LOUISE. What would you write, Helen? Tell us some juicy gossip.

HELEN. If I once open my mouth—

LOUISE. Come on, Helen, don't be a tease. I want to hear all the dirt.

HELEN. Dirt I leave to others to write.

LOUISE. Now don't cop out.

HELEN. (*To* JACK.) Cop in. Cop out. Do you know what she's talking about?

LOUISE. I want to hear about all the skeletons in your closet.

HELEN. Rattle. Rattle. Louise, I can't keep up with you. You want dirt? I'll tell you a dirty story. See, I can be as up to date as the rest of them. Listen my children and you shall hear!

LOUISE. This should be good!

HELEN. I was in Waldbaum's last week. A very respectable looking old man comes up to me and without so much as a by-your-leave he starts serenading me. Me with a shopping cart, him with a shopping cart, and he's singing me a love song! Eighty if he's a day! (*Sings.*) "If you were the only girl in the world and I was the only boy . . ." Can you imagine such chutzpa? He wasn't drunk either. Is that dirt enough for you, Louise?

LOUISE. Helen, I always suspected it. You're an old flirt.

HELEN. Girl, have you got the wrong number.

LOUISE. I don't know, Helen, I've always suspected you hide a juicy secret life.

HELEN. I've Got a Secret. (*To* JACK.) Do you know what she's talking about?

JAKE. O.K., that's enough, Louise.

LOUISE. What am I doing?

JAKE. You know what you're doing.

HELEN. I can go along with a gag.

LOUISE. Helen and I are having a pleasant chat. Why do you have to put your ten cents in?

JAKE. It's two cents.

LOUISE. Who cares?

JAKE. Try to get your cliches straight.

LOUISE. You worry about your own cliches. You're cliche enough.

JAKE. You're right. I'm wrong. Let's forget it.

LOUISE. (*To* HELEN.) He doesn't approve of the way I talk.

JAKE. I thought we agreed to forget it.

LOUISE. Oh, I can forget a lot more than that. You know what he decided to start a lecture on? (*Turns away from* HELEN.) You're a mother, Marilyn, you should appreciate this: He tells me I don't answer when Edie calls.

JAKE. Louise, she can hear you.

LOUISE. Big deal. He tells me I'm a terrible mother because when his daughter commands I don't flip to attention.

JAKE. You don't what? Flip to attention?

LOUISE. Flip to attention. Everyone knows what flip to attention means.

JAKE. Maybe they can interpret what it means, but you are not speaking English. It is simply not English.

LOUISE. Now what are you so upset about?

JAKE. I'm not upset.

LOUISE. I'd appreciate your not going to great length to make me look idiotic in front of company.

JACK. That's us, I suppose. We're "company."

LOUISE. (*To* JACK.) Don't mind him. I don't.

JACK. (*Rises.*) "The company" is going to visit his granddaughter.

JAKE. Don't, Dad. Her door is closed.

LOUISE. Then how could she hear me? (*To* MARILYN.) He should have been an English teacher.

JACK. So her door is closed.

JAKE. When her door is closed it means she wants to be alone.

HELEN. "I vaunt to be alone." Some house this is.

JACK. I come all the way from Riverdale to see my granddaughter and I can't see her because her door is closed. That's the most ridiculous thing I ever heard of.

JAKE. Dad, I know you don't respect privacy in *your* house but in this house we do respect it.

JACK. That's some hell of a remark!

JAKE. A closed door has never meant anything to you, has it?

HELEN. Listen, if we gave you all the privacy you wanted, to this day you wouldn't know a soul.

JAKE. All I'm saying is sometimes you need a little relief from other people.

JACK. I am not "other people" and I am not "company."

JAKE. She'll come out to see you when she's ready.

LOUISE. See what I mean?

JACK. I am her grandfather!

JAKE. In my entire childhood nobody ever knocked before they came into my room.

HELEN. What was so precious you had to hide from us?

JAKE. That's not the point.

HELEN. You were lucky you had a room.

JAKE. That also is not the point.

HELEN. Who paid rent on that room? That I ask you.

JAKE. O.K., but you're not paying rent on Edie's room.

HELEN. If we didn't pay rent on your room, Edie wouldn't have a room for you to pay rent on. I don't see why we have to put up with a show of temperament just because I bought her a book she doesn't want. She should learn to appreciate the thought behind the gift.

JAKE. Like you, I suppose?

HELEN. You can teach Louise English, I can still teach my son a few manners: Don't be fresh.

JAKE. Mama, you never knew how to receive a gift, how can you criticize Edie?

JACK. "Other people"? That really makes me see red!

JAKE. Never! Every single time I have ever bought you a present — I'd save pennies, nickels, dimes — what was your reaction? Every single time! "How much did it cost? When did you buy it? What do I need it for? Will they take it back?"

HELEN. It's not true.

JAKE. Oh, but it is true.

JACK. "Other people"! Where do you get off, Jake? I'm her grandfather, I'm your father, I knew you even before you were a big shot. Where do you get off to call me "other people"?

JAKE. You're other people to Edie, Dad, not to me.

JACK. Maybe if I saw her more than twice a year I wouldn't be "other people."

JAKE. You're seeing her now. Why do you always —

JACK. If I'm seeing her now, where is she? Point her out. You mean that closed door there that I can't knock on and ask if I can go in. Is that her? Is that what you mean when you say I'm seeing her now?

JAKE. No one said you couldn't knock and ask if you can go in.

JACK. I have your permission.

JAKE. You don't need my permission.

JACK. Thank you very much.

JAKE. All you needed me for was to introduce you to the concept of knocking on a door. (*Knocks on the table.*) It's easy, see? And then she says, "Come in," and you're not interfering.

JACK. You sure I won't be interfering?

JAKE. I'm almost positive.

JACK. I wouldn't want to interfere. (*Starts for* EDIE's *room.*)

HELEN. Jack, don't. It's very obvious you're not welcome.

JAKE. He is welcome.

JACK. You know what I think? I don't think he knows what he wants.

JAKE. Dad, I want you to knock on the door.

JACK. Thank you.

HELEN. Jack, don't.

JACK. Don't worry about a thing.

HELEN. I forbid it.

JACK. What's gotten into you?

JAKE. Oh, for Christ's sake, Mama!

HELEN. You don't have to knock on any doors. I won't put up with this humiliation.

JACK. I'm not humiliated, why should you be humiliated? All I want to do is see my granddaughter.

HELEN. Your problem is you have to be told when you're humiliated. Nothing changes with you.

JACK. You don't know what you're talking about.

HELEN. I forbid you to knock.

JAKE. Calm down, Mama.

HELEN. I hope you're satisfied, Jake.

LOUISE. Can everyone please calm down. Really, there's nothing to get hysterical about.

MARILYN. Take it easy, Louise.

LOUISE. Why should I be the one who has to be told to take it easy?

MARILYN. Because they can't help it and you can.

LOUISE. They don't want to help it.

MARILYN. Same thing.

LOUISE. So I have to shut up.

MARILYN. So don't shut up.

LOUISE. Everyone finds it so easy to give orders in my house.

MARILYN. I apologize for opening my mouth.

HELEN. You've got a lot to learn, Jake. You're going to spoil that child. You're going to have a lot of trouble on your hands in a few years, Jake, believe you me.

JAKE. Mama, I don't think you're necessarily the best source of advice on the question of child raising.

HELEN. I did so bad with my son?

MARILYN. I'm here too, folks!

HELEN. (*To* JAKE.) What's gotten into you? Is this the price of success?

JAKE. Mama, I know you think you did your best. But I also know how I felt. Are you interested in learning how I felt?

HELEN. Why should I be interested when I know it'll come out against me?

JAKE. I'll tell you anyhow.

LOUISE. Poor Jake.

HELEN. All children feel that way. You're not so special.

JAKE. Mama, you don't know how all children feel. You can't! Because you have never known how one specific child feels.

JACK. Who could keep up with all your moods?

JAKE. (*To* JACK.) You always take her side! When

Uncle Eugene gave me a watch for my fourteenth birthday—Mama came into my room—without knocking. (*To* HELEN.) You saw me holding the watch—my first grown-up watch, not a Mickey Mouse, a real seventeen-jeweled watch—(*To* JACK.) She took it out of my hands. I was fourteen but she just plucked it out and said, "This is a very expensive watch your uncle gave you, Jake. You must treat it with respect and care." And she started to wind it. You can't have forgotten this. She gave me a lecture on how to wind a watch. (*Throughout,* JAKE *is miming the winding of a watch.*) "You've got to be very careful, Jake, very responsible, once a day, don't overwind—" (JAKE *mimes the stem coming out of the watch, mimes* HELEN *looking down in shock at the stem in her hand.*) And out it comes, the stem! She runs to you in the kitchen reading your newspaper and she screams, "Look what Jake did!" Naturally, naturally you believed her. When it was a fight with strangers, you believed the strangers, so why not Mama? Between me and any grownup you believed the grownup.

JACK. You don't know what you're talking about.

HELEN. You did break it.

JAKE. It's a long time ago. It doesn't matter. I was using it as an illustration.

HELEN. You were playing with it; you loosened it, Jake. Sonny, why are you doing this?

JAKE. What I'm saying is don't tell me what Edie's going to have to deal with when she grows up.

JACK. I can't listen to any more of this nonsense. (*Looks for a door to leave by.*)

JAKE. Never once did you support me in anything. You know that's true.

JACK. Boloney! We support you all the time.

JAKE. After I made it on the *Times*! I had to make it with strangers in order to get accepted by my mother and father. Jesus Christ!

HELEN. You've gotten hard, Jake.

JAKE. What do yo think it feels like to be asked: "What's new?" all the time. "What's new?" "I was on page one of the *Times*," not enough. "What's new?" "I won the Pulitzer Prize—"

HELEN. Really! Oh, sonny boy!

JACK. Cut it out, he's not serious.

JAKE. No, I'm not serious, goddamn it! Christ, if I don't have anything new to report—

JACK. I'm ashamed I was proud of you. You want me to be ashamed? Well, I am ashamed.

JAKE. You don't get it, do you?

JACK. I get it. You want our support but you don't want us to be proud of you. It's very simple. What's not to understand?

JAKE. O.K., you want to know what's new?

JACK. I don't want to know. I'll never ask again.

JAKE. No, I'll tell you what's new.

JACK. I'm not interested.

JAKE. This morning, not an hour before you got here, Louise and I decided to separate.

MARILYN. Christ!

LOUISE. *You* decided.

JAKE. I decided. Tonight after you leave, I leave. That's what's new.

HELEN. Sonny!

JACK. You're a jackass! (*Turns away.*) I don't want to hear another word.

HELEN. Is this true, Louise?

LOUISE. Don't look at me. (*To* JAKE.) We agreed not to, Jake. (*To* HELEN.) I have nothing to do with this.

HELEN. Now I understand why the commotion. Jake, sit down, Jake. Come, sonny boy, sit beside me.

JAKE. Not now, Mama.

HELEN. This is a tragedy, Jake.

JAKE. It's no tragedy, it happens all the time.

HELEN. To your child, to your home? No, not all the time, sonny boy.

JAKE. One out of three marriages end up in divorce. That's a fact of life, not a tragedy.

HELEN. What's turned you so cold, Sonny, that you can talk this way after you do such a thing? Did Louise do something I should know about?

JAKE. Leave Louise out of this.

HELEN. Sonny boy, my heart is breaking. Please sit.

JAKE. (*Sits.*) Nothing happened. (HELEN *takes his hand.*)

HELEN. It's not that you don't want to tell me?

JAKE. You're on the wrong track, Mama.

HELEN. She didn't do the unmentionable?

LOUISE. Helen, I resent that.

HELEN. (*To* JAKE.) Don't tell me *you're* doing anything to be ashamed of?

JAKE. No, Mama, I am not screwing around.

HELEN. (*Withdraws her hand.*) Less talk like that and you might not be endangering your home. Jake, I'm no dope. I know what goes on. Be strong, sonny boy.

JACK. He'll do what he wants. Don't waste your breath.

HELEN. Whenever you had a problem we'd sit down, we'd talk it out.

JAKE. I'm not sixteen anymore, Mama.

JACK. Big shot!

HELEN. Who can you talk to if not your parents, Jake?

JAKE. Mama, this is pure fantasy on your part.

HELEN. (*To* LOUISE.) Louise—

LOUISE. He never talks to me.

HELEN. Why is he leaving?

LOUISE. He won't tell me.

JAKE. That's not true.

LOUISE. We really haven't talked at all about it, Jake. You know that's true.

JAKE. We talked all morning about it.

LOUISE. Well, I didn't understand a word you were saying.

JAKE. Because you don't know how to listen.

LOUISE. Because you don't know yourself, or you're not telling me the truth. If you want my opinion—

JAKE. You don't have to broadcast it.

JACK. Now we're a "broadcast"! He's got some gall!

HELEN. Calm down, Jack.

JACK. Never mind about me.

HELEN. Don't lose your breath. You look grey.

JAKE. Mama, will you stop implying that I'm killing him.

HELEN. You think this is doing him good? Two months out of the hospital. How often did you come around?

JAKE. Once a week.

JACK. One hour exactly. One hour he visits, then he can't get out of there fast enough.

JAKE. All you ever wanted to talk about was "What's new?"

JACK. I had a heart attack, what did you want me to talk about?

JAKE. We have never had a conversation in our lives.

JACK. Boloney!

JAKE. Every time I ask you anything about yourself you ask me "What's new?"

JACK. Who needs a reporter in the hospital? The way you ask, it's like it's going to be printed in the *Times*.

MARILYN. If anybody wants to know what I think, I think Jake and Louise should be left alone to settle this by themselves.

HELEN. Marilyn, be a good girl, get your father a cup of tea.

JACK. I don't want tea.

HELEN. Do what I ask, Marilyn.

JACK. I want a drink.

HELEN. See, Jake? Need I say more?

MARILYN. Scotch, Daddy?

HELEN. Marilyn, I forbid it.

MARILYN. One drink isn't going to make that much difference, Mumu.

HELEN. One drink, one curse word, one divorce. It all makes a difference, Marilyn, dear. Listen to me for a change, I wasn't born yesterday. Where are you going, I'm not finished.

MARILYN. Dad's not the only one who needs a drink. (*Exits.*)

HELEN. You too?! (*To* JAKE.) An epidemic! Weaklings! Is that what I brought up?

JACK. What's going to happen to that poor baby?

JAKE. That's our business.

JACK. I'm not talking to you.

JAKE. Edie is my main concern in this matter.

LOUISE. Naturally.

JAKE. I didn't mean you weren't my concern. I meant that you and I together would see that Edie came out of this all right.

HELEN. You can't tell her, Jake. Oh, Sonny—

JAKE. Mama, she has to be told why her father is moving out.

HELEN. Well, so tell her you're going away for a

while. To do research on a new book.

JAKE. There you go, Mama!

HELEN. You used to be such a beautiful child, Sonny. What's made you so selfish?

JAKE. Look, you don't understand. I didn't make this decision overnight. It is a matter of saving my life. Now does that mean anything to you, Mama, Dad? Saving my life? Then you might for once try giving me a little support. (*Mimicking commercial.*) "Try it, you'll like it!"

LOUISE. I've destroyed his life.

JAKE. I didn't say that.

LOUISE. You can't deny I always supported you, Jake.

JAKE. That's true, you have. It's more complicated than that.

LOUISE. Is that the only explanation I get? "It's more complicated than that"? That's all he tells me. I can't find a clue out from him. Do you want younger women? I'm willing to discuss it. I know about male menopause.

HELEN. I can't believe my ears.

JAKE. You will say anything in front of anybody!

JACK. Be careful! Don't "broadcast" to "other people"!

JAKE. Look, I did not mean for this to turn into a seminar on the subject of divorce.

HELEN. Divorce?! No, Jake!

JAKE. All I know is that I have to get out.

MARILYN. (*Enters with drinks.*) Dad.

HELEN. Defy me. Everyone defy me! (MARILYN *drinks.* JACK, *after some hesitation, drinks, starts to cough, chokes.* ALL *run to his side, slap his back, hold his arms up.* HE *finally recovers.*) Are you all right?

JACK. (*Weak.*) Fine.

HELEN. Lie down.

JACK. I don't have to.

HELEN. I'm not taking any more nonsense from you, young man. Lie down. (JACK *stretches out on couch.* HELEN *takes empty glass from his hand, looks at* JAKE *in disgust.*)

MARILYN. Don't look at Jake, Mama, I gave him the drink.

HELEN. (*To* JAKE.) I hope you're proud of yourself.

MARILYN. Mama, it's my fault, not Jake's.

HELEN. (*To* JAKE.) You'll ruin your life.

JAKE. You don't know the first thing about my life.

HELEN. How many times did we have to sit you down when you wanted to go off half cocked and talk some sense into your head?

JAKE. That wasn't sense, it was fear. All my life you have been able to reason me out of everything I wanted to do.

HELEN. Did we stop you from going on the *Times*?

JAKE. I hate the *Times*!

JACK. I can't believe it. I won't believe it . . .

HELEN. Sonny, why are you doing this?

LOUISE. Oh, let him have his fling. See if I care!

HELEN. Who's been putting ideas in your head, Jake?

LOUISE. You used to say I was the first person you ever met who supported you.

JAKE. In my work. In my work.

LOUISE. Oh, I see. Because I'm a rotten housekeeper.

JAKE. Must you, Louise?

LOUISE. An unworthy mother.

JAKE. You're a broken record, you know that?

LOUISE. Or is is that I'm not smart enough for your new friends?

JAKE. I need new friends, you got rid of all my old friends!

LOUISE. Screw you! You didn't like them anymore than I did!

HELEN. Children!

JAKE. I liked them fine until you started picking them apart!

LOUISE. Who gives a shit! You can have all the friends you want! Just don't see them around me.

JAKE. This happens to be my home. I'd like the freedom to invite my friends to my own home.

LOUISE. I suppose you don't hate my friends?

JAKE. But do I stop you from seeing them?

LOUISE. Because you don't have to be here!

JAKE. What's the use? They're not interested in this.

MARILYN. I don't think this is getting us anywhere. Mama, Daddy, I think it's time to go home.

JACK. I'll never ask him what's new again. That's a promise.

HELEN. (*To* JAKE.) He looks terrible. Look at your father.

MARILYN. Did you hear me? We are now going home. (*Puts down drink, goes to hall closet.*)

LOUISE. I couldn't go near you because you were working. What am I supposed to do? I have to talk to somebody.

JAKE. Every time I tried to read you a new paragraph I had to wait till you got off the telephone.

MARILYN. (*Her coat on.*) Is anyone coming with me? I mean it, I can't stand any more of this. I'm leaving. Who's coming?

LOUISE. That's all you ever do is read to me.

JAKE. You sure as hell don't read to yourself.

LOUISE. And if I don't like what you wrote you go crazy! You can't take criticism.

JAKE. It's the way you criticize!

MARILYN. O.K., folks. Mama, Daddy.

LOUISE. You have to admit I'm right most of the time.

JAKE. You can be right without being hostile!

LOUISE. I'm not hostile! I know you're going to jump down my neck!

MARILYN. The chauffeur has her coat on. Last call.

JACK. (*Sits up.*) You never could talk to him. I tried. He doesn't know what he's talking about.

HELEN. Lie down, Jack.

MARILYN. Would anyone like to say goodbye?

JACK. Who the hell do you think you are?

HELEN. Jack, mind your p's and q's.

MARILYN. No? I didn't think so.

JACK. The ingratitude! He deserves a piece of my mind.

HELEN. Only don't get excited.

MARILYN. (*Opens door.*) Thanks a lot. From now on take a taxi! (*Exits as* JACK *rises, crosses to* JAKE.)

JACK. How many times do you visit in a year? How many times? How many times? You're too damned important. Three times! Twenty-seven times in ten years!

EDIE. (*Enters.*) Mommy, I want you to see this. (*Holds book up.*) *The Cat in the Hat.*

JACK. (*To* JAKE.) Who'd believe it?

EDIE. (*Holds second book up.*) *The Cat in the Hat.* (LOUISE *ignores her.*)

JACK. (*To* HELEN.) Who'd believe it?

HELEN. It's enough!

EDIE. By Dr. Seuss. By Dr. Seuss. (LOUISE *takes her by the arms, holds her still.*)

JACK. (*To* HELEN.) Twenty-seven times in ten years!

HELEN. Jack, I forbid this!

JAKE. O.K.!

JACK. (*To* HELEN.) Other parents take credit! (*To* JAKE.) Did we ever take credit for your accomplishments?

JAKE. O.K.! You want to know about my accomplishments? I'll tell you one last "what's new."

JACK. Where do you get off? (EDIE *twists free of*

LOUISE, *crosses to* JAKE.)

JAKE. No, this you'll really be interested in.

EDIE. Dad, this is important. (*Holds book up to* JAKE.) *The Cat in the Hat.* Right? Now look at this. (*Holds up other book.*)

JAKE. Friday afternoon I gave notice at the *Times.*

EDIE. *The Cat in the Hat.*

JACK. You *what?*

HELEN. Oh my God!

JAKE. I am quitting the *New York Times!*

HELEN. Oh, Sonny, what's the matter with you?

JACK. Are you crazy? Have you gone crazy?

JAKE. I've quit!

HELEN. Oh, what a tragedy, what a tragedy!

LOUISE. Good riddance!

JAKE. It's too late!

JACK. I can't believe my ears. (*Looks at* LOUISE.)

LOUISE. Don't blame me!

HELEN. It's heartbreak! You're killing us, Sonny, you're killing us.

JAKE. Thanks for your support, Mama. Thanks, Dad. I really appreciate your support.

LOUISE. You bore me, Jake!

EDIE. You see, Dad, it's the exact same book. (JAKE *whips books out of* EDIE's *hands, holds them out of reach.*)

JAKE. (*Desperate.*) I can't, Edie! I'm quitting the *Times.*

CURTAIN

PROPERTY PLOT

ACT ONE
Right of Center:
Table
Chair left of table
Chair right of table
Chair center of table
On Table:
Chopping block and paring knife
On block:
   chopped red peppers
   chopped cabbage
   chopped onions
Salt and pepper mills
Parsley flakes
Downstage of Stove Counter:
Step stool

Stove Counter:
Below Stove on Counter:
Wooden spoon
Basket with rolls
Small bowl with parsley
On Stove:
Tea kettle with water
Two (2) copper pots
In stove:
Baking dish with chicken, covered with foil
Above Stove:
Two (2) hot potholders
Cookbook (open)

Sink Counter:
Stage Right Sink:
Bean salad
Stage Right Practical Drawer:
Potholder mitten
In Sink:
Rubber mats
Glass washer
(Check water on)
Under Sink:
Garbage can attached to stage right door
Above Sink:
Window closed
Stage Left of Sink:
One (1) glass
Plate of tomatoes
Can of olives
Can of artichokes
Dish towel
Practical Cupboard Stage Left of Sink:
(1) Parsley Flakes
(2) Minced Onions
(3) Oregano

Island Down Stage of Left Sink Unit:
On Island:
(1) Large plate with tomatoes
(2) Paper napkins
(3) Deviled eggs with cut up apple
(4) Dish with fish
(5) Plate with sandwiches
(6) Salad bowl with salad
(7) Small dish with parsley
(8) Chopping board

(9) Small bowl of quartered eggs
Stage Left of Island:
Stool
Stage Left of Door:
Stack of soda
Bags of pretzels on top of soda
In Refrigerator:
Bottle of salad dressing
Downstage of Refrigerator:
Bar Cart:
Bottle of ginger ale
Four (4) high ball glasses
Four (4) low ball glasses
Bottle of scotch (no cap) — practical
Three (3) bottles for dress
Bar towel upstage side of cart
Soda on bottom shelf

Off Stage Left:
Three (3) large bowls
One (1) large square basket
One (1) large oval basket
One (1) wooden salad bowl
One (1) teacup with water
In teacup — one (1) teabag inside of saucer
Tray with dirty glasses
Glass with ginger ale
Two (2) drawings

ACT TWO
Stage Right:
Desk and chair
Desk lamp stage right of desk

Waste basket stage left of desk
On Desk:
Holder with pens and pencils
Galleys
Yellow pad
Felt pen (open)
Phone
On Bookshelf Above Desk:
Jake's book cover
Stage Center:
Chair
Stage Left Center:
Chair

Stage Left:
Sofa
Ripped book (Miss Marple) in pocket of sofa
Upstage of Sofa:
Glass side table
On Table:
Lamp with removable shade
Box of kleenx
Ash tray
In Front of Sofa:
Coffee table
On Table:
Several magazines
Bowl with walnuts and apple
Book (Miss Marple)
Ash tray
Upstage Left:
Two (2) large plants

Edie's Room:
Desk with chair

School books on desk
Color crayons
Oak tag paper
School notebook
"Cat in the Hat"
Bed stage left
Stage right corner — 3 or 4 pillows
Assorted stuffed animals
Lamp above desk

SCENE CHANGE

Set:
Two large plants stage right
Bowl of flowers
Plant on coffee table

Strike:
Galleys and yellow pad from floor
Miss Marple from coffee table

Off Stage Right:
Tray with five (5) glasses with soda
Bowl with pretzels
Bowl with peanuts
Two (2) glasses with scotch
"Cat in the Hat" gift wrapped
Sweater in small shopping bag — sweater wrapped in
   tissue paper and bag folded over and taped

COSTUME PLOT

JAKE — Bob Dishy
Act One:
Blue blazer
Beige gabardine trousers
Blue/white stripe
Blue/red stripe tie
Cordovan loafers
Light grey
Watch
Wedding ring

Act Two:
Chinos
Blue V-neck sweater
Light blue short sleeve oxford cloth shirt
Topsider sneakers
Same socks
Same belt
Same watch
Same ring

Act Three:
Brown corduroy jacket
Tan wool trousers
Beige button down collar shirt
Same shoes as One
Same belt
Same ring
Same watch
Same socks

JACK — Hal Gould
Act One:
2 piece grey blue suit
Blue/white windowpane check shirt
Pattern bow tie
Dark grey socks
Brown shoes
Belt
Wedding ring
Watch
Handkerchief brown/white/blue

Act Three:
2 piece dark grey suit
White with red & black stripe
Maroon pattern necktie
Black socks
Black shoes
Same belt
Same ring
Same watch
Handkerchief blue & white
Overcoat
Wool scarf
Perk pic hat

HELEN — Frances Sternhagen
Act One:
2 piece bone knit suit
Lavender blouse
Grey open toe sandals
Nude hose
Slip & bra

Wedding ring
Engagement ring
Pinky ring
Watch
Pearls
Gold chain
Pink, purple, white beads
Purple/gold bracelet
Gold band bracelet
Pearl earrings
Sweater clip
Wig

Act Three:
2 piece pink wool suit
Beige blouse
Same jewelry
Burgundy overcoat
Navy clutch bag
Navy pumps
Same slip & bra
Same hose

EDIE — Jennifer Dundas
Act Two:
Blue jeans
Olive sweatshirt
Navy Addidas sneakers
Blue plaid knee socks
Blue/white barrettes

Act Three:
Navy print dress

Off white tights
Dance trunks
Black embroidered Chinese shoes
Same barrettes

LOUISE — Cheryl Giannini
Act Two:
Burgundy cotton sweater
Green/red/beige print skirt
Beige/green print socks
Grey slip on wedgies
Nude hose
Slip
Bra
Wedding ring
Gold chains

Act Three:
Maroon paisley dress
Sling back sandals
Same hose
Same bra
Same ring
Same chains

MARILYN — Kate McGregor Stewart
Act One:
Dark green print cotton dress
Rose canvas wedgies
Purple beads
Gold hoop earrings
Wedding ring

Nude hose
Slip
Bra
Tortoise hair combs

Act Two:
Teal turtleneck pullover sweater
Dark brown/green paisly shirt
Brown knee high heeled boots
Brown ultra suede vest
Tan overcoat
Burgundy shoulder bag
Gold shell earrings
Gold chain necklace
Same hose
Same slip
Same bra
Same ring

Other Publications for Your Interest

KNOCK KNOCK
(LITTLE THEATRE—FARCE)
By JULES FEIFFER

3 men, 1 woman—Composite interior

Take a pair of old Jewish bachelor recluses, throw in Joan of Arc who also in another life was Cinderella—add another character who appears in various guises and you have the entire cast but not the story of this wild farce. Cohn, an atheistic ex-musician is the house-keeper "half" of this "odd couple." Abe, an agnostic ex-stockbroker is the practical "half." They have lived together for twenty years—are bored to tears with one another and constantly squabble. Cohn, exasperated, wishes for intelligent company and on the scene enters one Wiseman who appears in many roles and is part Mephistopheles, part Groucho Marx. Then Joan of Arc appears before the couple telling them her mission is to recruit two of every species for a spaceship trip to heaven. After that all antic hell breaks loose and continues to the mad ending. ". . . a wild spree of jokes . . . helium-light laughter."—Clive Barnes, N.Y. Times. ". . . a kooky, laugh-saturated miracle play in the absurdist tradition."—Time. ". . . grand fun, possessed by a bright madness . . ."—N.Y. Post. ". . . a knockout of original humor."—NBC. ". . . intelligent and very funny play."—WABC-TV.

(Royalty, $50-$35.)

LITTLE MURDERS
(ALL GROUPS—COMEDY)
By JULES FEIFFER

6 men, 2 women—Interior

"Jules Feiffer, a satirical sharpshooter with a deadly aim, stares balefully at the meaning-less violence in American life, and opens fire on it in 'Little Murders.' . . . Can be devas-tatingly lethal in some of its coldly savage comic assaults." (N.Y. Post). The play is really a collection of what Walter Kerr called set pieces, showing us a modern metropolitan family of matriarchal mother, milquetoast father, normal cuddly sister, and brother who is trying to adapt himself to homosexuality. Sister's fiance is a fellow who knows how to roll with the punches; he figures that if you daydream while being mugged, it won't hurt so much. They have a hard time finding a preacher who will marry them without pronouncing the name of God. But they succeed, to their sorrow. For immediately afterward sister is killed by a sniper's bullet. A detective who has a stack of unsolved crimes suspects that there is "a subtle pattern" forming here. "'Little Murders' is fantastically funny. You will laugh a lot."—N.Y. Times. "You have made me laugh, you have made me collapse. I want to go back."—N.Y. Post. "One of the finest comedies this season.—NBC-TV.

(Royalty, $50-$25.)

Going Ape

NICK HALL

(Little Theatre.) Farce.
3 male, 2 female—Interior

This hilarious and almost indescribable farce has some serious undertones. Rupert, an idealistic and romantic young orphan, has come to his uncle's house to commit suicide. This proves to be no easy matter. For one thing he is constantly attended by his uncle's attractive nurse/secretary. He is also constantly interrupted by a stream of visitors, at first fairly normal, but increasingly incredible. Rupert realizes that all the visitors are the same three people, and his attention is drawn toward understanding the preposterously Victorian plot in which he is trapped, and which, in a startlingly theatrical climax, he begins to understand. "An intricate plot with subtle foreshadowing and a grab bag of surprises . . . some of the funniest characters you'll ever see molded into a tight dramatic package."— News, Fort Myers. "Every scene transcends not only the imagination, but melds into a literally death-defying whole. It's fast, like 2,000 mph . . . a play as old and as contemporary as today." Sarasota Journal. "Going Ape is truly zany . . . the wackiness is infectious." —Time.

(Royalty, $50-$25.)

Eat Your Heart Out

NICK HALL

(Little Theatre.) Comedy.
3 male, 2 female—Interior

In this theatrical comedy Charlie, an out of work actor currently employed as a waiter, takes the audience through a sequence of hilarious encounters in a succession of Manhattan restaurants. By changing the tablecloths during the course of the action the basic setting of three tables and six chairs becomes a variety of New York restaurants, both elegant and shabby. The scenes change, the action is uninterrupted and the comedy never stops. The other performers play several parts: the girl desperately trying to eat snails and oysters to please her fiance; the middle-aged couple whose marriage is breaking up; the lovers so intent on each other they cannot order dinner; the rich, embittered astrologer; the timid man who never gets a waiter; the agents, directors, actors, and waiters. An amusing gallery of characters whose stories intertwine and finally involve Charlie. The author of "Accommodations" has written a very funny, contemporary play that is also a serious comedy of backstage life. ". . . a sharp, stunning play. It'll make you howl—but better yet, it might even make you sniffle a bit."—Fort Lauderdale News. "Tightly written and very, very entertaining. I recommend it enthusiastically."—Miami Herald. ". . . About as good as anything I've ever seen in dinner theater . . ."—Fort Lauderdale Times.

(Royalty, $50-$25.)

Communicating Doors
ALAN AYCKBOURN

"A real knockout.... This is a show to see."—*New York Post*

"An inventive diversion."—*The New York Times*

This intricate time-traveling comic thriller by the British master of farcical comedy delighted London and New York audiences. A London sex specialist from the future stumbles into a murder plot that sends her, compliments of a unique set of hotel doors, traveling back in time. She and two women who were murdered in 1998 and 1978 race back and forth in the past trying to rewrite history and prevent their own violent deaths. 3 m., 3 f. (#5301)

The Dinner Party
NEIL SIMON

"A blizzard of one-liners.... The audience can bank on some good laughs."—*New York Daily News*

"Hilarious but also dangerously serious."—*New York Post*

Here is a decidedly French dinner party served up in a chaotic mode that only a master of comedy could create. Five people are tossed together in the private dinning room of an elegant Parisian restaurant for an evening that will forever change their lives. Playful antics, sudden zaniness and masterful comic dialogue punctuate the unfolding mystery. 3 m., 3 f. (#388)

Our *Basic Catalogue of Plays and Musicals* lists other comedies by Alan Ayckbourne and Neil Simon.

Send for your copy of the Samuel French BASIC CATALOGUE OF PLAYS AND MUSICALS

After Crystal Night
JOHN HERMAN SHANER

"Serious stuff, to be sure, yet its great
strength is its sustained comic tone."
Los Angeles Times
"Stunning, powerful, thought-provoking drama."
Christian Science Monitor

Seymour Goldstein's Beverly Hills household is in for an
emotion-packed weekend after he attends a meeting to deter-
mine if Jewish militants will be allowed to speak to his B'nai
B'rith lodge. Everyone in his family and those close to it
confront their roots and question their lives, history, future
and motivations, as well as the depths of their assimilitation
What could be the unraveling of an American Jewish family
turns out to be its salvation. 8 m., 2 f. (#3029)

Rose
MARTIN SHERMAN

Rose, played by Olympia Dukakis at The Royal National
Theatre in London and in a Lincoln Center production in
New York, is a survivor. Her remarkable life began in a tiny
Russian village, took her to the Warsaw ghetto, aboard a ship
called *The Exodus,* and finally to the boardwalks of Atlantic
City, the Arizona Canyons and salsa-flavored nights in Miami Beach. This one-woman show by the author of *Bent* is a
portrait of a feisty Jewish woman and a reminder of events
that shaped the twentieth century. 1 f. (#116899)

**Send for your copy of the Samuel French
BASIC CATALOGUE OF PLAYS AND MUSICALS**

Gripping Plays From
Ariel Dorfman

Purgatorio

A man and a woman enter a room. We see only a small bed, two chairs, and a table. Is it an asylum? A prison? Interrogation room? Questions are asked and answered. We feel we know the story. In this room, both the man and woman are faced with the truths of their lives. Are there crimes for which there can be no forgiveness? If there is no forgiveness, how do we move on with our lives? "Perhaps no ancient tale has inspired more debate or provoked more horror...a charged, poetic inquiry into human relationships that dangles the possibility of redemption just out of reach." Theatermania.com 1m, 1f (18715)

The Other Side

In a country at war for many years, a man and a woman wait. They pass their days confirming the identity of dead bodies at a hut near the border of the two fighting countries. When peace and a border guard arrive, chaos ensues. This moving and strangely comic work raises potent questions about war, identity, and love in our times. "Mr. Dorfman has set out to denounce the cruelty of global feuds fired by nationalism and ethnic prejudice."— *The New York Times* 2m, 1f (#17742)

For more of Dorfman's penetrating work, see

THE BASIC CATALOGUE OF PLAYS AND MUSICALS
online at www.samuelfrench.com

THE LADY WHO CRIED FOX!!!

(LITTLE THEATRE—COMEDY)

By EDWARD CLINTON

3 men, 2 women—Interior

When a jealous actor who's always on the road, finds out his wife has taken on a young male roommate to meet expenses, the show does not go on. He immediately returns home to find out what's going on. The roommate, an inventor who likes to roller skate, is caught in the middle between a jealous husband and frustrated wife. Eventually, all five of the characters get into the act and the result is just plain fun. ". . . punch and humor . . . a funny play. . . ." — Miami Herald. ". . . clever script . . . intriguing sense of humor coupled with a powerful knack for drama. . . ." —Fort Lauderdale News. ". . . funny, delightful and above all devoid of the off color material so many writers feel is essential. . . ." —Hollywood, Fla. Sun Tattler.

(Royalty, $50-$35.)

NOT WITH MY DAUGHTER

(LITTLE THEATRE—COMEDY)

By JAY CHRISTOPHER

3 men, 3 women—Interior

Will Gray suddenly has a problem. His 18-year-old daughter appears at his "swinging singles" apartment door. It seems Will and his neighbor, Rip Tracy, a velvet-voiced radio Dee Jay have a penchant for juggling girls like antacid tablets. Poor Will has a go-go girl in the living room—with her motor running—and a devoted young lady in the bedroom—but that's o.k. since she loves him. Rip has a girl in his apartment already when Will calls on him to also entertain the go-go girl. Then Will's daughter appears to complicate matters further—not only are explanations in order—but daughter has problems of her own. How it all is resolved will leave the audience limp with laughter. An adult play with not one leering joke. It's all in fun. "Funny? Absolutely." —High Point, N.C. Enterprise. ". . . a laugh riot . . ." —Greensboro, N.C. Daily News. ". . . fast-paced farce with as many laughs as you can handle in one sitting." —Lexington, Ky. Herald.

(Royalty, $50-$25.)

A COMMUNITY OF TWO
JEROME CHODOROV

(All Groups) Comedy
4 Men, 3 Women, Interior

Winner of a Tony Award for "Wonderful Town." Co-author of "My Sister Eileen," "Junior Miss," "Anniversary Waltz." This is a charming off-beat comedy about Alix Carpenter, a fortyish divorceé of one month who has been locked out of her own apartment and is rescued by her thrice-divorced neighbor across the hall, Michael Jardeen. During the course of the two hours in which it takes to play out the events of the evening, we meet Alix's ex-husband, a stuffed shirt from Wall Street, her son, who has run away from prep school with his girl, heading for New Mexico and a commune. Michael's current girl friend, Olga, a lady anthropologist just back from Lapland, and Mr. Greenberg, a philosopher-locksmith. All take part in the hilarious doings during a blizzard that rages outside the building and effects everybody's lives. But most of all, and especially, we get to know the eccentric Michael Jardeen, and the confused and charming Alix Carpenter, who discover that love might easily happen, even on a landing, in the course of a couple of hours of highstress living.

"Thoroughly delightful comedy."—*St. Louis-Post Dispatch.* "A joy."—*Cleveland Plain Dealer.* "Skillful fun by Jerome Chodorov."—*Toronto Globe Star.*

ROYALTY, $50-$35

ROMAN CONQUEST
JOHN PATRICK

(All Groups) Comedy
One set—3 Women, 6 Men

The romantic love story of two American girls living in the romantic city of Rome in a romantic garret at the foot of the famous Spanish steps. One of the world's richest young women takes her less fortunate girl friend to Italy to hide unknown and escape notoriety while she attempts to discover if she has any talent as an artist—free of position and prestige. Their misadventures with language and people supply a delightful evening of pure entertainment. Remember the movies "Three Coins in the Fountain" and "Love Is A Many Splendored Thing"? This new comedy is in the same vein by the same Pulitzer Prize winning playwright.

ROYALTY, $50-$35

Breinigsville, PA USA
11 March 2010
234060BV00004B/13/A